Sufism
The Essentials

D0838729

Sufism
The Essentials

Mark J. Sedgwick

The American University in Cairo Press
Cairo · New York

Contents

Introduction

In the West, there is a real and growing interest in Sufism, one of the world's most widespread and important religious paths. The beauty of the poetry of Jalal al-Din Rumi, the most popular Sufi author in translation, is clear to all, but the real nature of Sufism is not well known. Many of the best-selling Western texts on Sufism present a version of Sufism which is very different from that found in the Muslim world for at least the last millennium. These works often portray Sufism as something separate from Islam, which is simply not the case. While this author is not qualified to judge the spiritual worth of such "alternative" versions of Sufism, it is clear to anyone who knows Sufism from the Islamic world that they are a particular offshoot of Sufism, not Sufism itself.

Even without this problem, those who read Rumi so enthusiastically are not well positioned to reach an understanding of what Sufism is, though Rumi may guide them to understandings a Sufi would endorse. Rumi was not just a poet: he was a great shaykh, one of the dozen or so best-known Sufi masters whose names were perpetuated in the Sufi orders to which they gave rise, orders that still exist today. Rumi's prime objective, like that of any Sufi shaykh,

1

was the spiritual development of his own followers: their education in the outward, exoteric practice of Islam, but particularly their training in its inner, esoteric practices. Rumi's poems were ancillary to his main task: personally guiding people on the path which leads, in this world, to the One God before whom Sufis, Muslims, and many others believe they will stand on the Day of Judgment. His poems were originally addressed to an audience very different from a contemporary Western one: not only were Rumi's followers steeped in the teachings of Islam, exoteric and esoteric, but they were also embarked on a spiritual journey made possible by practices such as prayer and fasting, Rumi's guidance, and, for a Sufi most importantly of all, God himself.

This book cannot hope to put its readers into exactly the same position as that of Rumi's intended audience. More than words would be required for that. It aims, however, to give a basic understanding of the nature and history of Sufism, as it first appeared in the Islamic world and as it is today in the Islamic world and in many other countries, including Western ones. It concentrates on the earlier stages of the Sufi path, partly because these are the stages which the majority of Sufis who have ever lived have traveled. The higher reaches of the path have been trodden by relatively few. Some of those who have reached these higher levels have attempted to convey their experiences, sometimes in poetry and sometimes in symbolic or metaphysical abstraction, but such higher spiritual experiences are barely comprehensible to those who have not themselves approached them. This author does not consider himself qualified to write on them, and expects that most of his readers will be in the same position.

For most of Islamic history Sufism was of the greatest importance in the religious and social lives of most Muslims, and in economics and politics as well. Although it is today in partial eclipse in the Islamic world, it is still very much alive, and of small but growing importance in the West. It remains important today not only for many Muslims, but also for those non-Muslims who wish to understand Islam or Islamic societies. The face of Islam and of Muslims that is most familiar to Westerners today is not one that can easily be sympathized with. Strife, violence, and intolerance are what come first to the minds of many in response to the word 'Islam.' Those representatives of Islam whose activities result in the attentions of the world media are indeed often publicly committed to the use of violence to achieve their aims and are rarely noted for their tolerance. While seeing the West as their enemy, they complain of being treated as an enemy by the West—not a combination likely to win them much sympathy or support there. Fundamentalism, activist Islam, protestant Islam—whatever one wishes to call it—has roots in the traumatic experience of colonialism and the economic sufferings of many Muslim peoples, and in the collision between modernity and tradition. It also has important roots in the religion of Islam, but it does not represent that religion. Statistically, vastly more Muslims have been Sufis than Fundamentalists, and Sufism is (in the view of many, including the author) far more representative of Islam than is Fundamentalism. An understanding of Sufism is one of the best available routes into an understanding of Islam itself: not of the political ramifications of Islam, but of Islam as a lived religion—of the reality which lies at the heart of Islamic societies past and present, and so even (though arguably in dangerously distorted form) of the images of Islam so well known from our television screens.

3

1 What is Sufism and where does it come from?

The origins of Sufism

Nobody is entirely sure why Sufis are called Sufis. The etymology of the Arabic word *sûfî* is unclear. It may come from *sûf*, wool; there is a theory that a group of especially devoted followers of the Prophet Muhammad wore woollen cloaks, which were in those days cheaper and less comfortable than those in general use. Alternatively, the word may come from *suffa*, a raised platform or step, and refer to a group of particularly devoted Muslims who used to assemble on a platform outside the house of the Prophet. There are several other theories, none of them much more convincing than these two, and none of them particularly helpful, either. What all these explanations have in common, though, is a reference to special devotion and to the Prophet.

Many Sufis themselves, when asked to define a Sufi, will use a phrase such as "a traveler on the path back to his Maker"—defining Sufism in terms of its objective. Such definitions may be inspirational, but are not very useful to the historian or the sociologist. To confuse matters further, there are today Sufis who do not even describe themselves as

Sufis—they may describe themselves merely as pious or as followers of Shaykh So-and-So.

Certain non-Sufi Muslims are quite clear about what a Sufi is: a Sufi is a Muslim who has departed or been led astray from the path of Islam and is following practices borrowed from other religions. Views such as these, and the difficulties they have caused for Sufis, are discussed in Chapter Five, but are mentioned here because they have also been held by Western scholars, some of whom see Sufism as syncretism, an amalgam of elements of different religions. There are certainly syncretistic elements in the beliefs and practice of some Sufis, especially uneducated ones from poor and isolated communities, but then the religion of the poor and uneducated always differs from that of the educated and religious professionals, not only in Islam. A scholar in Damascus who has spent his life studying the central texts of Islam under a series of other scholars knows very well what is in them and what is not; a peasant farmer's beliefs and practices are derived less directly, and misunderstandings may more easily occur. In countries such as India, where Muslims live side-by-side with non-Muslims, the potential for transfer from one culture to another is high; similar transfer can also be observed in the other direction, for example, from Muslims to Arab Christians. Instances of syncretic transfer into the Sufism of the uneducated are to be expected, then, but it is easy (and wrong) to exaggerate the number of these instances of extraneous elements. Western scholar–administrators in Malaya, for example, observed in the nineteenth century that Sufis often visited graves and concluded that they had inserted Hindu grave-worship into Islam; in fact, Muslims of all varieties visit tombs in all parts of the Islamic world, including places such as Morocco, where Hinduism is not known.

All in all, that some elements of some Sufis' Sufism come

from outside Islam does not tell us much about the origins of Sufism. The view of Sufism as the product of syncretism does, however, throw some interesting light on Western scholarship: it is clear that this view originally derived partly from nineteenth-century racial theories. A once popular view saw the Aryan races as being gifted with imagination and creativity, and the Semitic races—principally the Jews and Arabs—as doomed to sterile legalism. For followers of this theory, Islam, like Judaism, was the legalistic product of the inferior Semitic mind; Sufism, more spiritual, could only have come from somewhere else—from the Aryan minds of the Persians, from outside Islam. The contrast between Sufism and Islam was taken so far that when a character in Kipling's *Kim* is described as a Sufi, this is glossed as 'a free-thinker,' which, as we will see, is not at all an accurate description.

As the view of Sufism as coming from outside Islam because Arabs could not possibly have invented it faded, the different preoccupations of a different century replaced it with another view. In the twentieth century a view of Sufism as the Islam of the people arose, of Sufism as vital and emotional and generally fun, as opposed to the dry Islam of the educated elites. Again, syncretism—but this time not from racially desirable Aryans, but rather from politically desirable oppressed classes. In fact, Sufis can come from any class, as is discussed in Chapter Two.

Sufism is sometimes wrongly seen as something akin to a philosophy and as rejecting the strict rules of Islam. Sufis are sometimes thought to be especially addicted to two forbidden fruits, wine and young boys—a view resulting largely from taking literally the images used in certain Sufi poetry, where intoxication and (male) lovers are often referred to. In these poems, intoxication in fact refers not to alcohol but to God, and the beloved represents the divine—the use of the male

7

gender to refer to presumably female lovers is a long-estab-
lished, if somewhat strange, tradition of Arabic poetry. If such
misreading were not possible, the metaphors of the poetry in
question would lose much of their force. There have been Sufi
orders such as the Malamatiya, whose name derives from the
Arabic word for 'blame,' whose followers deliberately broke
Islamic law in order to attract blame and thus avoid the risk
and difficulties of public adulation of their piety and sanctity. Such orders are, however, very unusual. The vast majority
of Sufis follow the *Shariʿa* (the rules of Islam) scrupulously,
perhaps more scrupulously than most non-Sufis.

The case for syncretism or philosophy as the origins of
Sufism, then, is far from proven. The difficulty with establishing alternative origins is that there is no mention of
Sufism in the earliest historical records of Islam. To some, the
significance of this is clear: Sufism must be a later invention.
Sufis themselves disagree. In a well-known phrase, many
Sufis will tell you that at the beginning Sufism was a practice
or reality without a name, and that now it is a name without a
reality. The 'now' can be today or centuries ago. Muslims, like
many others, see history as a decline from a golden age—the
golden age being in this case not Greece or Rome, but the
time of the Prophet. There are various recorded sayings of the
Prophet *(hadith)* which endorse such a view, speaking of the
inevitable decline of faith and standards over the centuries
which were to come after him. The companions of the
Prophet, according to some, were in fact all Sufis, and as a
result there was no need for any special label to describe
them. It was only as time passed and the Muslims fell away
from their original perfection that the group of those who
remained immersed in the depth and breadth of primeval
Islam needed a label—Sufis—to distinguish them from the
rest, who increasingly followed a more superficial religious

practice. This is a standard Sufi explanation of the origins of Sufism, and while it is impossible to prove scientifically, neither can it be disproved.

Sufism as a practical program

A more fruitful approach than attempting to understand Sufism in terms of its origins is to examine its objectives. In the last resort, these do not differ significantly from the objectives of Islam as a whole; what is distinctively Sufi is different emphases and special techniques. Chief among the objectives of Islam are submission to the will of God and to God's instructions, and preparation for the Final Day. This is a view with which no Muslim, Sufi or not, would disagree.

Submission is much stressed in Islam: indeed, the word *islâm* literally means 'submission,' and a *muslim* is one who has submitted. But while the emphasis in some religions is more on explanation than action—for instance, Protestant Christians tend to extract guidelines from general principles and apply them, as they wish, to their own actions—Islam generally emphasizes action far more than explanation. Rather than deriving action from principle, Muslims often deduce principles from instructions for action. In theory at least, a Muslim does something or refrains from doing it not because that seems sensible or right, but because that is what God has instructed. Although one may speculate about the *hikma*—the reason or wisdom behind an instruction—it is the instruction that counts, not the *hikma*. This does not mean that Islam looks only at actions, however. It is often said that we will be judged by our intentions—an interesting variation on the Christian proverb that the road to hell is paved with good intentions—and intentions are generally stressed throughout Islam: many ritual acts, for example, have no meaning or effect if performed without the requisite intention.

9

Sufism, then, aims at the submission of the Sufi to the will of God and at preparation for the expected meeting with Him, as does Islam as a whole. An essential element in this preparation is the control of the *nafs* or lower self. All Muslims agree on the need to subdue the *nafs*, but the emphasis given to the struggle with the *nafs* is distinctively Sufi. A *hadith* much beloved of Sufis talks of two types of struggle (*jihad*): the lesser *jihad*, against the enemies of Islam on the battlefield, and the greater *jihad*, against the *nafs*. This order is particularly significant when one remembers that the circumstances of the birth of Islam were such that the Prophet and his companions spent much time on the battlefield. This *hadith* is less frequently referred to in fundamentalist or political activist circles.

Nafs literally means 'self' and can also be translated as 'ego'—in the sense of 'egotistical,' not in the Freudian sense. It is the animal nature in man, that which drives us to eat, reproduce, lose our tempers, and fight. The objective is to control it more than to eliminate it altogether. In the image of one Sufi shaykh, the *nafs* is a like a powerful horse: if you can control the horse you can go many places, but if the horse is in control, you can achieve little. Sufis regard the *nafs* as a cunning but simple enemy, ever in waiting and easily influenced by Satan, but it is also an enemy which may sometimes be deceived without too much difficulty. The interior dialogue we all know as a struggle with temptation is seen by Sufis as a dialogue with the *nafs*, sometimes portrayed as a dialogue with Satan himself. All the arguments one might think of to justify eating forbidden fruit are the arguments of the *nafs* and should be ignored.

Sufism is best understood as a practical program for learning to control the *nafs*. Once the *nafs* has been subdued and a space made for God in the heart, God may be expected to fill that place with Himself, and ultimately the Sufi may come to know God while still on earth. This is described as *'irfan*, which may be translated as knowledge or gnosis. The path to *'irfan* is a long one, of course, and most Sufis never reach its end. Any progress along that path, however, is worthwhile, and the ultimate goal may usefully inspire even those who will never actually reach it. The techniques used by Sufis to move along that path and to subdue the *nafs* are considered in Chapter Two.

Orthodoxy, exotericism, and esotericism

Sufis distinguish for many purposes between the external and the interior, the exoteric and the esoteric. A verse of the Quran, for example, may have an esoteric or symbolic significance in addition to its plain meaning, its exoteric significance. This distinction is also applied to the *fiqh*, which is the exoteric rule of Islam. Esoteric and exoteric must be in balance: the right ideas are irrelevant if not concretized in action, and actions on their own serve little purpose. There is thus a greater tendency among Sufis to take a somewhat pragmatic view of the Law (the *fiqh*), to take into account the implications of an action in the struggle against the *nafs*—to avoid making a false idol out of the Law, remembering what it is for. This tendency is, importantly, to be found mostly among the shaykhs who lead Sufis, rather than in the Sufis who follow shaykhs; given the known cunning of the *nafs*, it would be a most dangerous proceeding for an individual to decide on his own to take a relaxed view of a certain injunction or prohibition. If one's shaykh tells one that in the modern globalized world economy there is little to be gained by worrying overmuch about paying interest on a house loan, that is another matter. From this greater-than-usual emphasis on the esoteric derives much of what is distinctive about the Sufi interpretation of Islam.

The existence of such an interpretation of Islam might imply the existence of an opposed non-Sufi or even 'orthodox'

11

interpretation. In fact, however, the Sufi interpretation of Islam is one view among many, along with modernist, liberal, and fundamentalist views, to name but a few. None of these are more or less authoritative than any others, partly because in Sunni Islam there is no single source of authoritative interpretation.

Most Muslims are Sunni Muslims, and it is with them that this book is primarily concerned. The largest non-Sunni minority within Islam, the Shia (nowadays most frequently found in Iran and Iraq) have a somewhat more authoritarian structure than most others, and offshoots of Shia Islam, such as the Druze or the Ismailis, do indeed have sources of infallible interpretation. Sunni Muslims, however, at the very most consider certain people better qualified than others to interpret Islam, whether because of greater learning, sanctity, or whatever. No one, however, is so well qualified that their interpretation is binding.

This situation might be expected to result in anarchy, but has not. This is because there is general agreement on the legitimate sources of Islam: the word of God recorded in the Quran and the *hadith*, the divinely-inspired instructions and comments of His Prophet, recorded in voluminous collections and studied by scholars and the pious ever since. There is also a general respect for the past consensus of the community of Muslims, in practice usually the consensus of the scholars among it. The Quran, for example, forbids the drinking of wine. The consensus of the community has been that whisky is much the same thing as wine; no one, therefore, can honestly maintain that the drinking of whisky is permitted. There has, however, been disagreement about coffee, tobacco, and hashish. The final consensus was that coffee was allowed. There has been periodic disagreement about the status of tobacco, and so in the absence of a consensus it remains possible to hold either view; much the same is true of hashish, though smaller numbers maintain that it is licit than defend tobacco.

Disagreement among Sunni Muslims is generally limited either to details such as these or to very broad questions of interpretation and significance, such as whether it is more important to ensure that a ruler is righteous or to avoid civil strife. Whatever views they may hold on particular matters, most Muslims who have ever lived were and are in agreement about most of Islam, and this large area of general agreement may be regarded as the 'core' of Islam, or even as 'Islam.' Descriptions such as 'Sufi Islam' or 'fundamentalist Islam,' then, refer to tendencies within Islam, and also tendencies within the groups in question. One might say, for example, that fundamentalists regard the struggle against illegitimate authority as a religious duty, while Sufis emphasize the struggle against the *nafs* or lower self. There are of course occasional Sufis who hold fundamentalist views on certain questions, liberals who hold occasional Sufi views, and so on. Since this is a book about Sufism, in areas where differences of opinion exist, 'Islam' will in general refer to a Sufi view of Islam.

The Sufi emphasis on the esoteric is one reason why Sufis are sometimes seen as quietist, withdrawing from the world. Another reason is the general Sufi reluctance to become involved in political activity; a favorite Sufi saying speaks of the desirability of neither knowing nor being known to the authorities. Involvement with the world, however, varies from order to order. Some orders have dressed their followers in old and patched clothes, while others have told people to dress well; some emphasize poverty, and some involve their followers in trade networks. The voluntary poverty of the followers of some orders gives rise to two terms often used to

describe Sufis: dervish (properly *darawish*) and fakir (properly *faqir*). The former of these words is of Persian origin,
used also in Turkish and Arabic and hence in European languages, while the latter is Arabic. Both merely mean 'poor,'
whether poor in a material sense or poor in spirit.

For most Sufis, the objective is to be withdrawn from the
world while living in it, to participate in life while not being
the slave of material concerns and desires (again, we return
to the *nafs*, which is of the world and loves the world).
Suspicion of those who take up with the powerful of the world
is almost universal among Sufis.

The first shaykh

For Sufis, the first shaykh was Muhammad ibn 'Abdullah
(571–632), known to Muslims as *Rasul Allah*, the Emissary
of God, and usually referred to in Western languages as the
Prophet Muhammad. The Prophet is not actually *called* a
shaykh or a Sufi, if only because there is no higher title than
that of *Rasul* and because the Prophet's role was much larger
than that of being the first Sufi, but no examination of Sufism
can start with anyone else.

The Prophet was born in Mecca, on the western side of the
Arabian peninsula, in the year 571. Although of an important
family, he was orphaned and brought up by his uncle, and
went through an early period of poverty before beginning to
make a good living as a long-distance trader. Mecca was at the
time an important urban center, intimately connected with the
nomadic tribes that surrounded it, but an urban society. It was
also a place of pilgrimage. A variety of deities were worshiped
at its central temple, the Kaaba, a small structure said to have
been built in remote antiquity by the prophet Abraham. It is
hard to form an exact picture of the society into which the
Prophet was born, since the details about which we know the

14

most are activities which Islam later put an end to, such as for-
tune telling, gambling, and the killing of unwanted female children. Certain varieties of manly virtue were evidently much
admired—amorous conquests, drinking, fighting, and long
trips through the desert on a beloved steed. The harsh moun-
tainous landscape around Mecca suggests that life was hard,
but more refined achievements were also respected, especially the art of the poet. The poetry which survives is in some ways
reminiscent of some Roman poets.

The Prophet was not at ease in the society which surrounded him and periodically withdrew into the desert to meditate.
It was while in retreat in a remote cave in the year 611 that the
forty-year-old Muhammad received his first revelation from
God, beginning with the words "Recite in the name of your
Lord!" This was the first of a series of communications which
were collected, some years after the Prophet's death, to form
the text of the Quran. Some of these communications are
directed to the Prophet, some to his followers, and some to
everyone; the totality of these communications is directed to all
mankind.

The Prophet slowly gathered around him a number of
Meccans, following him in the worship of the One God and
rejecting polytheism and the corruption of the society which
surrounded them. After some ten years, in 622, the opposi-
tion of those Meccans who did not follow him forced the
Prophet and his companions to leave Mecca. The early
Muslims then established themselves instead some three
hundred kilometers to the north, in the lush oasis city of
Yathrib, later renamed *al-madina al-munawwara*, the
'Illuminated City,' Medina. This emigration is known in
Arabic as the *hijra*, and the Muslim or *hijri* calendar starts in
the year of the *hijra*.

It was in Medina that the following of the Prophet expand-

15

ed and the Muslim community established itself; it was from Medina that the Prophet raised the armies which after several years of battles and skirmishes finally conquered Mecca and cleansed the Kaaba of idols in 630; it was in Medina that the Prophet died and was buried two years later, at the age of 61.

The Quran is the central text of Sufism, as of Islam. It is not, for Muslims, a work of the Prophet, but of God Himself, expressed in the language and terminology of the place and time, but coming from outside time and space. As the recipient of the revelations which became the Quran, the Prophet was little more than a messenger, though of a particularly elevated variety—hence the title *rasul*. The work of the Prophet himself was the establishment of the religion of Islam and of the community of Muslims. Islam was largely established by the personal example of the Prophet, and how a Muslim should live is thus defined as how the Prophet did live. Contemporaries' reports of what the Prophet said on particular subjects or did under particular circumstances were therefore collected and recorded, and these *hadith* reports are thus the source of much of the religion and law of Islam. The relationship between the Quran and the *hadith* is that the Quran usually speaks in general terms, of the importance of prayer, for example. Details—such as *how* to pray—are taken from the practice of the Prophet, the Prophetic *sunna* or tradition, recorded in the *hadith*.

The message of Islam which the Prophet taught had a variety of elements and covered most aspects of human activity, though in varying detail. It dealt with God's nature and purposes; with how and why to worship Him; with how to live; and with commercial and criminal law. How to live and how to worship are intertwined: certain acts are purely worship, such as the proper way of visiting the Kaaba, but few acts include no element of worship. Activities such as eating, going to

16

sleep, or washing all had elements of worship included in them. The numerous accounts of the Prophet teaching and answering questions may shed light on matters such as the proper rate of tithe on a particular type of agricultural land or what to do if someone starts the Pilgrimage and is then prevented from completing it by *force majeur*. In many reports, however, the Prophet describes the virtues which God loves and the acts that He hates. The virtues are sometimes virtuous actions and sometimes states of mind or of the soul. These reports are the basis of all of Islam's ethical teaching.

The Prophet is by definition the most perfect of men—the beloved of God, the knower of God, the successor to earlier prophets such as Abraham and Moses and Jesus, the final prophet who brought and taught the final message, valid and sufficient until the end of time. As the perfect man, the Prophet is also the perfect model. All Muslims since have tried to imitate him, in varying degrees. Some merely follow the most important of the rules he taught, while one pious man is said never to have eaten watermelon because although he knew that the Prophet ate it, he did not know what the Prophet had done with the pips. This story need not be taken entirely literally, but it indicates the extent to which imitation of the Prophet can go.

The Prophet was the first Sufi shaykh in the sense that he led his companions toward God by the most direct path conceivable. That personal guidance is not of course available to later Muslims, but a Sufi follows a shaykh who follows the Prophetic *sunna*; the more closely the shaykh follows the *sunna*, the more similar to the Prophet the shaykh becomes. Even the shaykh who resembles the Prophet most is not actually the Prophet, of course. To have the opportunity of following the Prophet himself, in the society which he himself established, which has been the prototype of all Islamic societies ever since—no Muslim and no Sufi could ever ask for more.

17

Two great Sufi theorists

Although Sufism is a practical program rather than a theory, and although great Sufis are most frequently remembered for their sanctity, teaching, or even poetry, Sufism does have its theorists. To compose a definitive list of the great theorists of Sufism would be hard, but two men immediately stand out: the Iranian moral philosopher, Muhammad al-Ghazali (d. 1111), and a Spanish cosmologist, Muhyi al-Din ibn al-'Arabi (1165–1240). Their writings have been and remain extremely influential, although no Sufi order traces its origins to them. Their works (along with the Quran, the Prophetic *hadith*, and various lives of saints) might occupy a Sufi embarked on the early stages of the path back to God or reaching its end.

Al-Ghazali was born in 1059 in Tus, Khorasan (northern Iran, then still a Sunni area). He initially studied the *fiqh*, in effect the codified portion of Islamic Law and at that time the standard education of a future scholar or administrator. He worked for some years as a *faqih* or jurist, and then in 1095, at the age of thirty-six and while occupying an important teaching position in Baghdad, he turned from the exoteric sciences to what he called the "real" sciences, the esoteric sciences of the human soul. He spent the rest of his life simply, returning home to Khorasan after travels in Syria and Palestine, and died in 1111 in the town of his birth.

He left behind many writings, of which the most important and best known is the voluminous *Ihya 'ulum al-din*, the Revival of the Religious Sciences. This meticulously organized work is divided into four sections, the first dealing with worship, the second with conduct in other areas of life, and the third and fourth with vice and virtue. Each section is made up of a number of books, dealing with questions ranging from types of knowledge to pilgrimage, marriage, pride, hope, and, finally, death. On each subject he deals with, al-Ghazali examines how

18

a Muslim should act and think, and then explains why, giving where possible a quotation from the Quran, a reference to the Prophet or, when all else fails, his own explanation.

The influence and popularity of al-Ghazali's work derive partly from its encyclopedic nature and its clarity, but also because his own explanations, although offered only as a poor substitute where what the Quran and the Prophet have to say is not immediately self-explanatory, come together to form a coherent exposition of Islam as a system for fighting the *nafs* and opening a space for God. It is this system and the emphasis on explanation that constitute the main difference between his work and the thousands of other works, before and after, dealing with similar questions. Other works tend to be more legalistic, either merely stating rules or perhaps discussing the relative merits of alternative interpretations in a dry fashion which might be informative, but which is hardly inspirational. Centuries later, al-Ghazali's work continues to convey to almost all who read it a remarkable feeling of conviction, strength, and purpose. Al-Ghazali's work is the point where the esoteric emphasis of Sufism meets with and illuminates the exoteric law of Islam.

Our second great theorist, Ibn al-'Arabi, was born in Murcia (southern Spain, then part of the Islamic world) in 1165. After studying in Seville, he traveled to Mecca in 1202 at the age of thirty-seven, and after periods in Cairo and Konya (Turkey) he settled in Damascus, where he died in 1240.

His two most important works were *al-Futuhat al-makkiya*, 'Meccan Illuminations,' and the shorter *Fusus al-hikam*, 'Bezels of Wisdom.' Neither of these are easy works, as is indicated by the reaction of a Jordanian shaykh when a young man came to ask for his comments on a proposed reading list during the 1980s. The shaykh crossed Ibn al-'Arabi off the student's list, saying "no one understands Ibn al-'Arabi any more." When the

19

student had left, another follower of the shaykh said, "But you are reading Ibn al-'Arabi with me!" "Yes," replied the shaykh, "and sometimes I'm not sure that I understand him, either."

Difficult as they are, Ibn al-'Arabi's works are indisputably of the greatest importance—not for the average Sufi, perhaps, but for those Sufis with an interest in the nature of the esoteric world. Ibn al-'Arabi explains the origins of the material world in the substance of the Prophet, who was made of light; he talks of the varieties of heavens and hells, of the numbers and names and ranks of angels; he maps the path back to God and speaks of the ultimate union of the mortal with the divine, of *wahdat al-wujud*, the Unity of Being. This concept has been one of the most controversial to arise in the history of Islam, being seen by its detractors as a variety of pantheism or even polytheism—a great evil in Islam as in any monotheistic religion—and by its enthusiasts as the key concept which facilitates passage through the final veil which separates creation from the Creator. Many have since attempted to explain it, justify it, or even to modify it. Since any explanation would take up the whole of a book considerably longer than this one, and since the realities Ibn al-'Arabi describes are anyhow largely incomprehensible to those who have not experienced something like them already, we will merely note the importance of this work for a minority of Sufis. Those interested will find suggestions for further reading in the bibliography.

Al-Ghazali and Ibn al-'Arabi are only two of many Sufi writers, but are the most important. Sufis see men such as these not as the originators of Sufism but as its transmitters. One can certainly find many similar ideas in earlier periods, in the case of Ibn al-'Arabi, most famously with al-Husayn al-Hallaj (858–922), who described his own experience of the higher end of the Sufi path by saying, "Ana al-Haqq"—"I am

20

Truth"—"Truth" as used here being one of the names of God. "If a piece of iron emerges from the fire red hot and says 'I am fire,'" asked a later commentator, "how should one take that statement?" The authorities of tenth-century Iraq were in no doubt and executed al-Hallaj for the grossest blasphemy.

The historical origins of the ideas of al-Hallaj, Ibn al-'Arabi, and al-Ghazali are as unclear as the origins of Sufism itself. One can work backwards until one finds the first written reference to something, but it is hard to state with certainty that the first written reference to something is the first occurrence of something. The reader, then, may make up his own mind, either to regard Sufism as originating with Islam itself and being subsequently refined and systematized by its practitioners, or as something resulting from the endeavors of theorists over the four centuries after Islam.

21

2 How to be a Sufi

Sufism and social class

Anyone can be a Sufi, whether rich or poor. Sufism in the twentieth century is certainly found more frequently in villages than in cities, and university graduates are rarely Sufis, but this was not always so. In the eighteenth century, almost any Islamic scholar or dignitary would be a Sufi, and an attack on Sufism was an attack on the religious elite. In the nineteenth century, the Ottoman Sultan 'Abd al-Hamid was not only a Sufi but an enthusiastic patron of Sufism, partly because he saw Sufism as a counter-weight to the various new trends which would soon lead to the replacement of the Ottoman empire by a secular Turkish republic in the twentieth century, but also for entirely altruistic reasons. In the twentieth century, individual Malay sultans and Islamic dignitaries may be Sufis, but they usually keep quiet about it in the face of reformist hostility, discussed in Chapter Five.

As has been said, Sufism is sometimes seen as 'popular' religion. Certainly, the Sufism of the educated and the uneducated differs as much as everything else about them differs, which is rather more in Islamic societies than in contemporary Western societies. A 'popular' version of Sufism exists, but

Sufism is high culture as well as low, represented by volumes of the finest poetry as well as songs composed by the uneducated, by works of philosophical abstraction as sophisticated as anything the West has produced as well as by half-understood superstitions. The relative absence of Sufism from the life of the rich in many contemporary Islamic countries parallels the relative absence of religion as a whole; for various reasons, the *concierge* of an apartment block in a rich part of town is far more likely to be found praying or reading the Quran than are most of those whom he serves, and a university professor is far more likely to ignore the Ramadan fast than a bus driver.

Educated Sufis in major cities will usually follow different shaykhs from peasants in villages, but sometimes a shaykh may count among his followers both the educated and peasants. At times, a scholar may follow a virtual illiterate, if the holiness of the illiterate is clear enough. Beyond this, the more educated and peasants will intermingle on certain occasions, especially the *mawlid* festival celebrated each year for the anniversary of certain great saints of the past.

Mawlids are occasions almost without parallel in the West, save perhaps in the Latin *fiesta*. The major *mawlid* of the year celebrates the birth of the Prophet, but many saints are also commemorated in the same way. In Cairo, the tombs of the great saints are mostly in the old city, in the old cemeteries, or around the Azhar university mosque. The old city is today a very poor area, with once great houses broken up and occupied by a number of poor families. For several days a year, a particular quarter of the old city around a mosque will fill with people celebrating the *mawlid* of the saint buried in the mosque, which often gives its name to the quarter in question. Some saints are more popular than others, and sometimes these *mawlids* are low-key affairs. Some are major events, however, and on these occasions tents will be erected by various Sufi orders, and local people may distribute free tea in the streets. Peasant families will come in from the countryside several days in advance, camping on blankets in the streets and making tea on spirit burners. On the night of the *mawlid* itself, people of all classes and types will come from all parts of the city. At the tomb of the saint, serious Sufis will celebrate the saint's life and deeds; at the extremities, people will test their luck and skill at fair stalls. In between, people will mill around and enjoy the festive atmosphere. It is said by Sufis that all, whatever their intentions, are the guests of the saint; one might add that all are equally welcome, whatever their origins—and indeed to some extent, whatever their religion. The *mawlid* is an excellent example of the all-inclusive aspect of Sufism.

Sufism and gender

Anyone can be a Sufi, man or woman. Almost all Sufi shaykhs are men, however, and many Sufi orders do not admit women, or admit them only to some associate status. To understand this, we must first consider the wider question of gender in Islam. Sufis are Muslims and generally live and operate in Islamic societies.

The whole question of gender in Islam is a vexed one, with Muslim women generally being seen in the West as oppressed and suffering. Some Muslim women do undoubtedly suffer, but it is incorrect to see Islam as uniquely or solely oppressive. The worst sufferings of Muslim women do not derive from Islam, but from economic circumstances, or from an individual's cruelty or stupidity, as elsewhere. Suffering may also derive from cultural factors independent of religion. The culture of Islamic societies should in theory derive purely from Islam, which provides a total system for every aspect of life, but in practice many other factors have influenced the

25

development of these societies, and the practice of a particular society on a particular point may often have little to do with religion, and sometimes even directly contradicts religion.

A rather extreme example of the divergence between Islamic law and the practice of some cultures is the response to premarital sex, which is forbidden by Islam. Islamic law specifies the same penalty for unmarried men and unmarried women: severe beating, but only if ordered by a court which has accepted the testimony of no less than four witnesses to actual sexual intercourse. In places such as the remote villages of the south of Egypt, however, a woman who is found in circumstances far less compromising than those required by Islamic law will be killed by her own relatives without reference to a court, as required by essentially tribal codes of honor, while the man involved may suffer no penalty at all. Islamic law does not recognize these tribal codes and regards such killings as murder, but local custom in practice takes precedence over Islamic law, even though it should not. Islamic law, in fact, gives women rights and protection which might not impress a contemporary Western feminist, but might have seemed more acceptable in 1914, in which year, for example, few European women enjoyed the unrestricted property rights of their Muslim sisters. That Islamic law offers much of value to women is indicated by the extent to which its provisions in these areas are generally ignored when they disagree with local custom.

At its best, the position of some women in contemporary Islamic societies does not differ much from the position of some women in the West in the 1930s, or may even be better. In Cairo, for example, female university graduates from well-off families study, travel, and follow careers much as they do in the developed world. They usually find their own husbands, and although home and children are then clearly their responsibility, they often continue to work, and relief from domestic duties is provided by servants (in the absence of labor-saving machines). At its worst, among the very poor, the position of women can be hard indeed, as can the position of men, of course. The poorly-paid maid of the university graduate who has just left for a medical conference in Germany may be attempting to support a sick mother, several children, and an unemployed husband.

What concerns us here, however, is not so much the position of women in the Islamic world, but in the practice of Islam. Here, gender matters far less. Both male and female Muslims expect to stand in naked terror before God on the Day of Judgment. The steps to take in preparation of that day, a day when differences of gender will not be on anyone's mind, are essentially the same, although some details of individual practice vary very slightly—men and women place their arms slightly differently when praying, for example, and men have no equivalent of the female exemption from fasting when pregnant. Gender is otherwise irrelevant to individual religious practice.

Gender differences, however, become apparent when it comes to communal practice. Most obviously, mosques tend to be male preserves. The congregation for the Friday Prayer is overwhelmingly male, since women are allowed to pray at home, while men are not. Since a woman may lead only other women in prayer, prayers in a mosque are almost invariably led by a man, although any women present may follow the prayer in a separate area. The extent to which such areas are provided varies according to circumstances; for obvious reasons, little provision will be made in an army camp, while equal provision will generally be made at institutions where numbers of men and women are approximately equal. On weekdays, women are to be found in the areas of office blocks

27

or university campuses set aside for prayer as much as men are, while mosques in the streets tend to remain dominated by men. Public religious ceremonial, then, is essentially male-dominated, as is the leadership of Islam. In this, Islam differs little from religions such as Catholic Christianity.

In questions of gender, Sufism follows Islam, and Sufis do not differ fundamentally from the societies in which they live. A Sufi man's first duty is to support his family, and a Sufi woman's first duty is to her home and children, exactly as for any other Muslim. A shaykh will be a man, just as the person leading group prayer will be, and when a female is a shaykh (or, properly, *shaykha*), she will lead only women. Communal practices such as Sufi ceremonies in mosques are led by men, as are all other activities in mosques, and women attending them keep separate from the men as they do on all other such occasions. Women, however, may follow a shaykh in their private practice, just as a man may, and just as men and women follow Islam in the same way on other occasions.

Sufism is, however, one of relatively few areas of Islam where women sometimes rise to prominence. One of the greatest literary records of the Sufi experience was written in the eighth century by a woman, Rabia al-Adawaya of Basra (Iraq), for example. Shaykhs are often succeeded by their sons on their death (for reasons discussed in Chapter Three), and in the absence of a suitable son a daughter may occasionally take her father's place, although it is more frequent for the daughter's husband to become the new shaykh. In Beirut, a branch of the Dandarawi order (discussed in Chapter Five) has since the 1970s been led by a female university professor who is not related to any past shaykh and who has provided a sort of *crèche* on the order's premises. But this unusual example may tell us more about the slow arrival of modernity in the Middle East than it does about Sufism.

The shaykh as exemplar

Anyone can be a Sufi, whatever their social class or gender, so long as they follow a Sufi shaykh. As has been explained in Chapter One, the first Muslims followed the example and the teaching of the Prophet as well as the word of God revealed as the Quran, and all Muslims since have attempted to follow the example of the Prophet, as recorded in a variety of texts and as codified into a variety of rules. The Sufi follows the Prophet like any other Muslim, but he also follows the living example of a man who, as much as possible, himself embodies the example of the Prophet. As was remarked above, the more closely someone follows the example of the Prophet in every act, word, and thought, the more closely that person comes to resemble the Prophet, and the more perfect an example that person becomes himself. The shaykh is, for a Sufi, the living exemplar.

In Catholic terms, a shaykh is perhaps described as a variety of bishop. It is often said that there are no priests in Islam, but in a certain sense it would be more accurate to say that all Muslims are priests. In the Catholic church, the performance of rituals is in general reserved for priests; laymen may attend Mass or a wedding, but cannot perform either. In Islam, any Muslim can perform any ritual (though in modern times the state tries to reserve the power to marry people to itself). In the same way that bishops can do certain things that ordinary priests cannot, however, a shaykh can do certain things that an ordinary Muslim cannot: most importantly, he can admit someone into a Sufi order or pass on to someone else the power to admit someone into a Sufi order. There is also a variety of apostolic succession in Sufism: any shaykh can tell you his *silsila*, the chain of shaykhs taking him back to the original human source of it all, the Prophet, who provides the ultimate link to God.

29

A *silsila* is the documentation of the authority of a shaykh, and every member of a Sufi order knows part of his shaykh's *silsila* and may be able to recite all of it. Most *silsilas* are by now very long—they have to go back more than 1,400 years—but some are shorter. As recently as the nineteenth century, shaykhs have received the command to start a new order from the Prophet in a dream, which results in a relatively short *silsila*. Transmissions of this sort between people who cannot have met in the normal, physical sense are not uncommon—one or two of the links in most *silsilas* are *uwaysi*, 'spiritual' transmissions of this sort.

A shaykh, then, is someone with a *silsila* who accepts those who wish to start on the Sufi path into the order which he heads; he 'gives' them the order. Sometimes he will be notable for his piety and holiness, sometimes for his learning, and sometimes for his ancestry alone. There are tens of thousands of shaykhs in the Islamic world at any one time, and not all of them are equally remarkable. How a shaykh becomes a shaykh is discussed in Chapter Three, but generally there are two ways. One is that one of the followers of an existing shaykh becomes so pre-eminent in some respect that he is authorized to accept people into the order himself, and then attracts large numbers of followers, possibly in a geographical area where his shaykh does not himself already have a following. At some later point, usually on the death of his shaykh, he himself may then become shaykh. Alternatively, in the absence of such a candidate after the death of a shaykh, the bereaved followers will often choose as their new shaykh a son of the dead shaykh or sometimes the husband of a daughter if there are no suitable sons. In this way, dynasties of shaykhs come to be founded, with the order passing from son to son for several generations. Generally, however, the great shaykhs under whom orders spread and grow are not sons of shaykhs, but students.

Some shaykhs have thousands of followers and some dozens. Sometimes the dozen followers may all be very serious followers of Sufism, many of whom later found orders of their own. Sometimes a shaykh has thousands of enthusiastic followers who devote themselves to the Way he is showing them, or sometimes the thousands may have only a vague allegiance to their shaykh. Participation in Sufism varies considerably.

Range of participation

The greatest Sufis are generally *walis*, a term which has so far been translated as 'saint,' but which differs in important respects. A *wali* is someone who is close to God, under God's special protection, and subject to God's special favor. No one knows who is really a *wali* except God Himself and perhaps some other *walis*. There is no equivalent of a canonization process, and the recognition of someone as a *wali* is a spontaneous popular process, which may sometimes be wrong. Ibn al-'Arabi once prayed to be shown the greatest *wali* of his age and was guided to a blacksmith's shop; the unknown man working at the forge turned to Ibn al-'Arabi, smiled, and raised his finger to his lips to indicate the need for silence.

Not all *walis* are known as such, but a *wali* may be recognized by the ability to work miracles or, strictly speaking, *karamat* (beneficences) which God grants him. Many stories of *karamat* are told of great shaykhs. These stories serve an inspirational purpose, but also confirm the legitimacy of the position of the shaykh in question. They vary from the dramatic—even raising people from the dead—to the mundane—throwing an empty bottle onto a railway track in such a way that it lands exactly upright on a rail. To some extent, the *karama* is in the eye of the beholder: some events which might strike a believer as a *karama* would merely strike a bystander as coincidence. In the Sufi view of the world, however, God's presence is so immediate that strictly speaking there is no such thing as a coincidence.

Wali is a spiritual rank, not to be confused with the function of shaykh. Not all *walis* are shaykhs, and not all shaykhs are *walis*, though perhaps most are considered to be *walis* by their followers. The rank of *wali* is in the gift of God, although a Sufi may take various steps to prepare for that rank. It is sometimes said in the hagiography of a shaykh that after many years of struggle and spiritual exercise, "his *nafs* died." This is one definition of the end of the Sufi path: a separation from the flesh while still alive, which will often be rewarded by God with extinction in God, with the experience of Him of which Ibn al-'Arabi, especially, wrote. Put differently, the various veils of creation which separate man from his Creator are pierced, and man beholds God. A man who has thus experienced the divine may well become a *wali*. Since the rank of *wali* is in the gift of God, an ordinary person may suddenly and unexpectedly be raised to it.

A *wali* has *baraka*, a term which cannot be exactly translated into European languages, but which lies close to grace or blessing, a variety of spiritual power. *Baraka* can hardly be felt, but both feeds and protects those who receive it; it is a concept present throughout Islam, but particularly important for Sufis. *Baraka* is present in food cooked with love and good intentions, but not, probably, in fast-food hamburgers. It is present in a *wali*, by virtue of his closer than usual connection with God: the blessings with which God showers the *wali* spill over to reach those close to him. It is present in a *wali* even after his death, and a visit to the tomb of a *wali* may produce *baraka* in the same way as a visit to a living *wali*. *Baraka* can be transmitted by intention ("bless you!") or acquired by physical proximity or, particularly, physical contact. Crowds will strive to touch the clothes of a *wali*, and visitors to a tomb will rub their hands against the metal rail around it. It can also be passed down a *silsila*, from shaykh to shaykh, and be acquired by entering an order. Some Sufis enter (or 'take') many orders, although they normally follow only one shaykh at a time. An order may thus be 'taken' for real guidance ('for the path') or as a sort of honorary degree ('for the *baraka*').

The end of the Sufi path, then, is mystical union with God, and the greatest Sufis are *walis* who have experienced this proximity to God. Most Sufis, however, do not fall into this category, and most do not encounter dramatic spiritual experiences that can be expressed only in poetry or allegory. Most Sufis are ordinary believers with a special thirst for the divine, for something more than the day-to-day practice of Islam can provide. Sufism may provide access to spiritual experiences which they would not otherwise have and provide a framework for their practice of Islam in a society which many see as only nominally Islamic, but the higher reaches of metaphysical abstraction are not very relevant to them. Most Sufis, then, are ordinary, but pious, people. Within this category, the degree of commitment also varies considerably, from the intense devotion described below to something more restrained.

Some Sufis are not even particularly pious. The tradition of belonging to a particular order may become established in a family or locality, and habit may thus bring people back to particular rituals or to visit a shaykh on special occasions—to ask for advice on a difficult problem, for intercession, or perhaps for a lucky name for a newborn child. Some such people may not even have formally 'taken' the order of the shaykh they half-heartedly follow, and some may not even call themselves Sufis; they merely 'know' that Shaykh So-and-So is someone to whom they can turn when in trouble, or that it is generally good and uplifting occasionally to spend time in his company and that of his followers.

The meaning of 'Sufi,' then, is very flexible. A Sufi may be a *wali* or someone on the way to becoming a *wali*. Often, a Sufi may be little more than a more or less pious Muslim. At the other extreme, a Sufi may be an occasional participant in activities he barely understands.

Essential practices

Sufis follow many practices, first and foremost among which are the standard practices of Islam—the five daily prayers, fasting, and so on. Sufis are usually more scrupulous in these standard observances than are many non-Sufis, and may add to them elements of their own. All Muslims, for example, are obliged to perform the ritual prayer at dawn, noon, mid-afternoon, sunset, and after sundown. Prayers which are missed must be made up later, and there are virtually no circumstances under which it is legitimate to miss a prayer. Despite this, many Muslims do ignore (and some almost certainly always have ignored) the daily prayers, and may perhaps only pray when they go to the mosque on Friday, or only during the month of Ramadan, or only in periods of personal anguish or uncertainty. The Sufi who routinely misses the daily prayers is rare indeed, and many Sufis add to the obligatory units of prayer extra prayers which take as long as or longer than the obligatory prayer (as of course do many pious Muslims who are not Sufis).

Fewer Muslims omit the Ramadan fast than ignore the daily prayer, unless they have some recognized excuse, such as being infirm or pregnant. This is partly because of the social nature of fasting: not only is it hard to break the fast without people knowing, and hard to find food or drink outside one's own home during the hours of daylight, but the breaking of the fast each evening is a communal and social activity from which few would wish to exclude themselves. Sufis, however, are more likely than most to observe addi-

34

tional voluntary fasts, perhaps on Mondays and Thursdays of
every week in the two months before Ramadan, perhaps for
six days during the month after Ramadan while everybody
else is relaxing. Once again, so do many pious non-Sufis.

In addition to the normal practices of any Muslim, which,
as we have seen, a Sufi may perform more carefully and more
frequently, Sufis have a variety of practices of their own.
Some orders are especially known for one practice or another, but certain practices are common to the vast majority of
orders, and so may be said to be truly Sufi. The most important of these are discussed below. Many are not, in the strict
sense of the word, 'religious practices' at all, but rather
aspects of the way a Sufi lives or a Sufi order works which
have the same spiritual results as formal practices do.

Love of the Shaykh

A Sufi follows a shaykh and loves his shaykh. The degree of
emphasis on love of the shaykh varies from order to order,
and in some cases is more explicit than others, but all Sufis
love their shaykh to a greater or lesser extent. This is so even
if the shaykh in question is dead, as a shaykh's own original
shaykh normally is.

In its fullest form, a Sufi's love for his shaykh is a form of
devotion, similar to a child's love for its parents: though the
term is not used in Islam, a shaykh is indeed a variety of spiritual father. When a Sufi is away from his shaykh, he will talk
about him with the same delight as anyone displays when
talking about someone they love, bringing them and what
they have said into any conversation whenever possible,
exhibiting for general delight details which to an outsider
may seem commonplace. The number of photographs of his
shaykh on display in a Sufi's home may outnumber those of
his own family, and occupy pride of place there; such photo-

graphs may also be found in his office and perhaps his car as well. When a Sufi is with his shaykh, all his attention is focused on him, and the smallest gesture of favor toward him on the shaykh's part is a source of immense delight. Many Sufis live far from their shaykhs, visiting them only a few times a year, perhaps traveling for many hours to do so, and nowadays in some cases covering half the globe for the purpose. For such Sufis, the week or so a year spent with their shaykh is more real and more important than all the rest of the year put together. This love is itself of spiritual benefit. Unlike love between man and woman or of a parent for a child it is altruistic, with no element of self-interest or desire to possess. It is a pure giving, a pure sacrifice of the *nafs*.

Love of the shaykh is coupled with obedience to and imitation of the shaykh, both of which are made easier by love. Obedience to another is a necessity when following a spiritual guide, but is also useful in itself: the *nafs* likes to obey no one, and so the habit of obedience to another is an effective subduer of the *nafs*. Sometimes a shaykh is obeyed in obviously spiritual matters: pray so many cycles of this formula every night, do not worry too much about something or other. A shaykh is also obeyed in other matters. A Sufi will normally ask his shaykh's permission to do a variety of things, most importantly marrying and traveling. Normally a shaykh's permission is felt to confer a type of blessing on such an action, but that permission is not always forthcoming. A Sufi may sometimes be denied permission to marry or divorce, or to move to another country; a Sufi may even sometimes be told to live in a certain place or do a certain job. A Sufi may even be given commands which have no purpose other than to test, and so strengthen, his obedience and thus to subdue the *nafs*. A Sufi's obedience to his shaykh is an exception to the general rule discussed in Chapter One that there is no one source of authoritative interpretation in Islam;

for a Sufi, his shaykh's authority is total, and his shaykh is almost infallible.

Imitation of the shaykh has obvious benefits. As has been said, the shaykh is himself following the *sunna* of the Prophet and imitating the Prophet, and so he who imitates the shaykh is thus imitating the Prophet, but with a nearer, more visible model. Imitation of the Prophet is compliance with the will of God, and the sequence shaykh → Prophet → God is found not only in imitation, but also in love. In loving his shaykh, a Sufi is ultimately loving God. Imitation also closes off a fertile field for the *nafs* to make trouble. A Muslim may, for example, be wondering whether or not to wear a beard. The Prophet wore a beard, it is *sunna* to wear a beard, but in most Muslim countries today people are generally clean-shaven; wearing a beard may not only be against an individual's inclinations, but might even draw the hostile attention of the police, who associate beards with subversive Islamist fundamentalists. The *nafs* may therefore find many good reasons to ignore this *sunna* and remain beardless. Alternatively, there is a more subtle danger: the decision to wear a beard despite all may swell the *nafs* with pride at obstacles overcome. For a Sufi, none of these problems are present: the shaykh wears a beard, so the follower will wear a beard also.

The Sufi may imitate his shaykh in wearing a beard or in getting up at dawn to pray the morning prayer on time (rather than praying it late, as many do); he may also imitate his choice of footwear or the dishes he eats. To an outsider, this can often seem very strange, even excessive. Great love often produces effects which seem excessive to the outsider, and the reverence shown to certain shaykhs by certain followers has sometimes been felt to be beyond that which any man should show another. Not every shaykh is treated thus by every follower, but while most Sufis will kiss the hand of their shaykh, some will also

kiss his feet; some will not turn their backs until they have left
his presence, walking backwards as if from a medieval king.
There is indeed something of the medieval court about the
house of many shaykhs: twenty to a hundred or more men sit-
ting around waiting for the shaykh to appear, filling their time
with stories of what he has just said or done, or with rumors of
what he might be about to do. The shaykh appears, and everyone rises. The shaykh is going into the town—five happy persons are selected to accompany him. He is going to pray in the
mosque—all may accompany him. He has gone—the initial
disappointment of the follower who has missed the chance to
accompany him is tempered by the reflection that this must be
how it was meant to be, and reduced by the anticipated joy of
seeing him again in the evening.

A Sufi's love for his shaykh is perhaps the most important
thing in his life. At the least, it is what binds him to his
order, to the practice of Sufism. In Sufi stories love for the
shaykh is often represented as being instantaneous: I saw
him, and I knew I loved him. It may precede or follow an
individual joining an order, but it is almost always present.
Such love is also an important factor in many older stories,
of the first Muslims' meetings with the Prophet.

An individual, in fact, does not really join an order: he
joins himself to a shaykh and to the shaykh's *silsila*. This
takes place in a ceremony which is more or less elaborate,
depending on the order, and which is in many cases known as
baya (the same word that was used for the oath of absolute
loyalty given to the Caliph of Islam, a swearing of fealty and
obedience unto death which has its parallel in medieval
Western kingship). Such a giving of allegiance is not under-
taken lightly, though often—when someone has felt immediate great love for his shaykh—it is done more than willingly.
In some orders, a shaykh will only accept *baya* after a period

of trial. The obvious trial is the tests which the aspirant follower must surmount, but the period of trial is also a trial in itself, in that the aspirant may have the opportunity to get to know his future shaykh: to love him or to decide that he is not the right shaykh.

The Sufi's love of and total obedience to his shaykh carries with it certain obvious dangers. It has happened that shaykhs have shown themselves unworthy of the love bestowed on them, particularly in the case of the love of female followers, which can acquire inappropriate carnal elements. Such scandals are, however, extremely rare—surprisingly rare, perhaps, given the nature and extent of the power a shaykh wields. This may be because it is hard for a charlatan to become a shaykh. It may also be because the roles of the shaykh and the follower are bounded by well-known limits, and an order normally operates in public; there is an important difference of opportunity here between a Sufi order and a Western cult.

If scandals resulting from a shaykh's abuse of his followers' love and obedience are exceedingly rare, scandals resulting from a followers' misunderstandings are more frequent, though still unusual. A Sufi's love of his shaykh may be so great that he begins to conceive of, and perhaps speak of, his shaykh as being some other figure from Islamic eschatology: the expected *Mahdi*, the divinely-guided one who will come at the end of time, or even the Prophet himself. Shaykhs do what they can to quieten the fantasies of their followers, but sometimes with little success. The one point on which a shaykh will often be disbelieved by his followers is his claims to a low spiritual rank.

This love and devotion is not found to the same extent in every case. What we have described is the love of Sufis for a great shaykh, for a shaykh who is also a great *wali*. Even in this case, different degrees of commitment are found with different

39

followers. For one, the shaykh will be the most important thing in his life; for another, the shaykh will be one of the most important things; for another, the shaykh will be merely important. Not all shaykhs are great shaykhs, and in the case of a Sufi who follows a shaykh out of habit as part of a local tradition, the love of the shaykh may be weak indeed, often replaced by a mixture of awe and respect. Awe and respect are of course present in the love we have described, and awe and respect on their own have something of the same effect, though on a reduced scale.

Community

We have seen how important a Sufi's love of his shaykh is, and also that in many cases a Sufi will only spend one week a year in the company of his shaykh. Even then, the amount of time a Sufi actually has alone with his shaykh is minimal. Popular shaykhs have little privacy, and a Sufi may at the most hope for a suitable opportunity to ask his shaykh a question in public at some point during a week. An actual discussion is unlikely, and a private discussion almost unknown for an ordinary follower. The person with whom a Sufi spends the least amount of time, then, is his shaykh. Much more time is spent with other Sufis, with other followers of his own shaykh or even of other shaykhs. This environment also plays an important role in the Sufi's spiritual training and progress.

Much unspoken testimony is paid by Islam to the influence of environment, and the concept of community is well established. The *umma*, the community of all Muslims, is much spoken of, and has some significance in reality as well. For at least the last thousand years, the *umma* has not been all that it might be, to the extent that some radical Islamists recommend a *hijra* away from corrupt society to re-establish a pure *umma*, on the model of the Prophet's *hijra* (emigration) from Mecca to Medina. Few go so far as this, but there is a general recognition that the

40

umma today—or at any point in recent centuries—is very different from that established by the Prophet, and from how it should be. As a consequence, visiting the *salihin*—those who keep to the straight path, the virtuous—is a recommended practice. Spending one's time with the *salihin* and avoiding places frequented by *fasihin* (wrongdoers, the corrupt), such as bars, means that one spends one's time with the better elements of one's contemporary, albeit imperfect, *umma*, and hence that one is living in something closer to the original *umma*. A gathering of Sufis is by definition a gathering of the *salihin*, or at least includes few *fasihin*. Living very much in the community of one's fellow Sufis, then, is a kind of internal *hijra*, away from the imperfect *umma* of later centuries.

Sufis spend time with Sufis for a variety of reasons, perhaps the most important of which is that people of common interests and views tend to associate anyhow. There are numerous occasions on which Sufis gather together: the *dhikr* (considered below), various *mawlid* celebrations (discussed above), and probably a weekly meeting often known as a *dars* or a *suhba*. A *dars* is a lesson, a *suhba* a meeting for purposes of companionship, and whatever the meeting is called, it usually shares characteristics of both of these. It may start with a talk of some sort, given by the shaykh or by someone else who is qualified to speak; the talk is invariably followed by tea and conversation among the Sufis present; in some cases, those who have assembled together may then eat together. These meetings are conducted on premises belonging to an order (a *zawiya*), in a mosque, or in the house of a shaykh or a follower.

These occasions on which Sufis may gather have greater significance than a Westerner might expect, because other occasions for people to meet are comparatively rare. The social life of Islamic countries in general revolves around the family, and visitors to a household tend to be either relatives or very

41

old friends. Parties on the Western model are virtually unknown, although the number of weddings of distant relatives a Muslim attends is probably similar to the number of parties a Westerner attends. Restaurants tend to be eating houses for working men rather than places one goes with family or friends, and cafes are similarly a male preserve and usually fairly basic in their amenities. Few of the many varieties of societies and clubs which occupy the spare time of many westerners exist. The various gatherings of Sufis, then, provide an unusual opportunity for sociability.

For a Sufi to spend much of the spare time he spends away from home with other Sufis creates, then, an environment which is sympathetic to the aims of Sufism and of Islam. Just as a Western drug addict may find it difficult to escape his habit because his established social life revolves almost exclusively around drugs, so a Sufi finds it difficult to stray from the right path because he is deeply enmeshed in a Sufi community.

Some orders take steps beyond the various gatherings already discussed to enhance the coherence and significance of the Sufi community. At one point it was common for Sufis to dress distinctively, most frequently in a *khirqa* or patched cloak, and 'taking the *khirqa*' came to be synonymous with joining an order. Some orders require their followers to wear a *sibha* (a plain wooden rosary) around their necks. Such badges or uniforms, in creating a distance between the Sufi and the surrounding society, obviously enhance the homogeneity of the Sufi sub-community. In more recent times, some orders have involved their followers in commercial activities; in some countries, it is still usual for some or many of the followers of a shaykh to live in an agricultural settlement, a variety of commune where all work together in the fields, on building new houses, or whatever. Other orders have used the network of their followers as trading networks. Commercial involvement or communal living with one's fellow Sufis is an effective way to build or maintain a sense of community, and so to provide an environment favorable to the practice of Sufism and of Islam.

Dhikr and wird

Much of the practice of Islam is designed to make people mindful of God, not to forget Him, to make people act consciously rather than automatically. When a pious Muslim of any variety says "b-ismi-Llah" (in the name of God) as he starts a meal or even begins to drink a glass of water, the objective is not just to remember that these are gifts from God, but to take these gifts thinkingly, rather than to respond semi-automatically to an urge of the *nafs*, as an animal does.

The Arabic for 'to remember' (in the sense of 'not to forget') is *dhakara*, and one use of the imperative form—'idhkur Allah,' do not forget God—is sufficiently widespread to have been chosen to adorn a number of signs on the motorway which links Mecca with Medina. The traveler or pilgrim on this road is periodically admonished, by signs that look very much like regular road signs, to give thanks to God and not to forget Him.

These signs are a Saudi peculiarity. More general is the use of repetitive prayer: one is unlikely to forget God while actually addressing Him. This variety of practice is found in most religions; many Catholics were once devoted to the rosary, for example. In Islam, repetitive prayer is known as *dhikr* (from the verb *dhakara*, its objective); the actual physical rosary is known as a *misbaha* or a *sibha* and consists either of thirty-three plain wooden beads or of three groups of thirty-three beads. The *sibha* is found throughout the Muslim world and is used by non-Sufis as well as Sufis. Sufis use their *sibhas* for counting repetitions of short prayers assigned to them by their shaykh. Normally, a given formula must be repeated a certain number of times a day: 100, 250, whatever. One Syrian housewife, finding frequent interruptions made it hard to keep track on a normal *sibha*, turned instead to a mechanical counter of the type used by museum guards to count entering visitors: "there is no divinity other than God," click, "there is no divinity other than God." It is counting that matters—not how one counts—so that the *nafs* cannot play tricks on one, to ensure that one does one's daily assignment, or *wird*.

The *wird* has many benefits, but for some orders a major objective is that the Sufi's constant repetition of whatever formula is used for *dhikr* should ultimately become an unceasing repetition, so that the formula repeats itself inside the Sufi's head and heart without interruption, whatever the Sufi is doing, perhaps even in sleep. When this is achieved, the Sufi in question is most unlikely to forget God. This technique is probably rather more effective than the Saudi road signs.

Different shaykhs assign different *wirds* and may also assign different varieties of *wird* to different followers, but the assignment of some *wird* is almost universal. The daily *wird* typically consists of certain longer prayers to be said and some *dhikr* to be done after the Dawn Prayer, some more *dhikr* or prayers after other Prayers, and some *dhikr* for any time during the day. The *wird* is the central, basic, distinctive practice of the followers of any shaykh.

As we have seen, community is also an important part of the practice of any order. As the *wird* (with its component of individual *dhikr*) is the basic individual practice, communal *dhikr* is the basic communal practice. The followers of any shaykh will gather at least once a week to do *dhikr* together. This meeting for communal *dhikr* goes by many different

44

names and takes many different forms, but all have in common that the followers of a shaykh are doing together on one
occasion what they do individually on many occasions.

One possible form of communal *dhikr* consists of a shaykh
and his followers, probably seated in a circle, possibly after
the Sunset Prayer on a Thursday evening (as in Judaism, in
Islam days run from sunset to sunset, so Friday starts after
sunset on Thursday). Toward the start of the *dhikr*, the shaykh
may for example say "*Ikhlas* [the name of a short chapter of
the Quran] ten times"—and everyone then recites the chapter in question, silently, ten times. The later elements of the
communal *dhikr* are usually shorter, more like the individual
dhikr, perhaps twenty-five repetitions of "Ya Rahman!" O
Merciful One! (*Rahman* is one of the ninety-nine names by
which God has made himself known.)

This type of *dhikr* is restrained and may appear rather
low-key. An observer of *dhikr*s might proceed from this basic
model by stages to the more spectacular models of *dhikr* (a
Sufi usually remains with one shaykh and so with one variety
of *dhikr*). The first stage is that a shaykh's followers may say
the *dhikr* aloud rather than to themselves; they may move
their upper bodies a little to the rhythm of the words. The
dhikr may be chanted rhythmically rather than said; the
movements may be more pronounced. The chanting may
become musical; the followers may stand, perhaps in lines
rather than a circle, and sway. Persons with particularly fine
voices may lead the chanting; drums or cymbals or pipes may
be introduced; the swaying may become swinging. Finally,
persons with fine voices may be replaced by a professional
munshid (reciter) who uses a microphone and an amplifier,
and who might even sell his performances on cassette tapes.
Swaying may turn to whirling; live snakes may even make
their way into the *dhikr*. In general, the more spectacular

45

*dhikr*s at one end of our scale are associated with shaykhs with more popular followings, and the more restrained ones at the other end with shaykhs with more educated followings, though this is not an invariable rule. I have seen doctors and professors swinging to Sudanese rhythms I could not myself follow, though I have never seen such people getting involved with snakes. Snakes are a peculiarity of one particular order, the Rifaʿiya; whirling is the preserve of the Mevleviya, once a major Turkish order.

The more spectacular *dhikr*s are also public spectacles, serving a secondary purpose of attracting new followers, while the more restrained *dhikr*s are commonly private affairs. This has the incidental effect of leaving many non-Sufis, especially Westerners, under the impression that Sufism is about snakes and whirling, because snakes and whirling are very visible, while a small group gathered in someone's house may be inaudible as well as invisible. The prominence of 'whirling dervishes' in the Western imagination has led the aggressively secular Turkish republic to export performances of the Mevlevi *dhikr* as a variety of 'folk dance'; the Egyptian Ministry of Culture subsequently sponsored regular performances in Cairo derived from this 'folk dance.' This enjoyable entertainment, known to foreigners in Cairo as 'the Sufi dancing,' has only a tenuous connection with real Sufism.

Communal *dhikr*, then, serves a variety of purposes. Like individual *dhikr* in the *wird*, it prevents its participants from forgetting God. It also brings all the followers of a shaykh together and thus enhances the unity of the community in question. Finally, it is a starting-point for new Sufis: passers-by who stop to watch a spectacle, perhaps join in, and perhaps return next week. A Sufi whose friend has expressed an interest in Sufism may take that friend to a *dhikr*, in the case of the more restrained *dhikrs*, normally after obtaining his shaykh's permission to bring a stranger.

Khalwa

A practice which has grown less frequent in recent years is *khalwa*, withdrawal. Sufis in general withdraw from the world while remaining in it, but they will sometimes withdraw from it totally as well. A shaykh may instruct a Sufi, at a particular stage of his spiritual development, to withdraw from society for a given period, often forty days. Some older *zawiyas* (the premises of an order) have cells built for this purpose; other orders may use caves or remote places. In general, during a period of *khalwa* a Sufi will leave his place of retreat only to attend the five canonical prayers in the mosque or to use sanitary facilities. Food will be delivered to him, and he will probably speak to no one, save for occasional meetings with his shaykh, during which he may discuss his states of mind, tell of his dreams, and so on.

Some Sufis follow more dramatic ascetic practices, either by withdrawing for longer periods or by depriving themselves of sleep. Such practices are however unusual and usually restricted to those on the very highest stages of the path back to their Creator. In the nineteenth and twentieth centuries, even normal *khalwa* has become less and less frequent.

Sufis, as has been said, withdraw from the world while remaining in it. They devote themselves in total obedience to a shaykh whom they may meet only comparatively rarely, but whose picture they carry with them wherever they are, perhaps literally on the dashboard of their cars or perhaps in their hearts. They perform an internal *hijra* to the virtual community of other Sufis and do their *wird* as they go about their daily life. They are in the world, as Muslims should be since the Prophet specifically forbade monasticism, and they have jobs and spouses and children; but in certain ways they are as much withdrawn from the world as a Christian monk, even without any actual *khalwa*.

The *majdhub*

An important exception to the general rule that Sufis are withdrawn from the world while remaining in it is a category known as *majdhub*, 'attracted'—taken by God toward Him. To an observer, many of the *majdhub* might simply seem mentally disturbed, but Muslims distinguish carefully between *majdhub* and *majnun* (taken by the jinn [spirits], possessed; in modern usage, crazy).

A *majdhub* might look crazy, but he is not. A *majdhub* is one who has been taken by God and who has not fully returned to earth. This state of *jadhb* (attraction) may be temporary or long-term. While in it, an individual is not fully accountable for his actions and may behave very strangely indeed. During a temporary state of *jadhb*, a Sufi may foam at the mouth or jerk like an epileptic. Such states are often seen during a *dhikr* of a less restrained variety, though in the more restrained varieties *majdhub* is normally discouraged and rarely seen. In extreme cases, a *majdhub* may jump into water and need rescuing, or faint, or scream. When *jadhb* is prolonged, the *majdhub* may become in appearance like a tramp, may talk to his walking stick, or may speak in tongues in an incomprehensible language known as Suryani, a language which sounds like no other human language.

The *majdhub* are in general treated with care and respect. This may be either a consequence or a cause of the in many ways gentle attitude of Islamic societies toward those with disabilities. Islam is one of the few cultures in which a blind person can rise to a position of prominence and in which it is quite normal for a scholar to be blind. There are few other large cities in the world where a simple-minded man may be allowed to roam at will with a large notice sewed to the back of his robe giving his name and address, as sometimes happens in Cairo. Respect for the apparently simple-minded may be enhanced, however, by the possibility that the afflicted is not only *majdhub* (and so under special divine protection) but even, perhaps, a great *wali*, someone who is to be feared as well as respected. Respect for the *majdhub* has at times been great enough for their details to be recorded in biographical dictionaries along with scholars, high officials, and *wali*s of a more normal variety. The archetypal dervish of the western imagination—poor, disheveled, and a little crazy—is *majdhub*.

To be *majdhub* is not, on the whole, regarded as desirable. Transient *jadhb* may be a blessing, since who would not want to be drawn by God toward Him? To be left permanently in a state of *majdhub*, however, is something of a misfortune, though awareness of their ignorance of divine purposes would restrain most Muslims from stating unequivocally that it was pure misfortune. Stories are told of a Sufi who anticipated his shaykh's instructions and undertook advanced spiritual exercises for which he was not prepared, of his sufferings in a prolonged state of *jadhb*, and of his final restoration to normality by his shaykh at a later period. Continuance of a state of *jadhb* is, then, a variety of occupational hazard for the Sufi traveler on the higher reaches of the path—infrequent, but spectacular.

49

3 The orders

The archetypal Friend of God

All Sufi orders since the eleventh century have been named after one of a small number of great shaykhs. These shaykhs may not have actually established the orders named after them in an organizational sense, but in each case an order emerged from the group of followers who were left on their death. Generations of shaykhs and ordinary Sufis have since acted in the name of one of these shaykhs and on the particular pattern he established. It can never be established with total certainty that the great shaykh from whom an order derives was a *wali*, but it is hardly possible that he was not. The start of any order, then, is the birth of the man who will become a *wali*, and so we will start our consideration of the orders with a composite biography, a picture of the archetypal Friend of God.

The birth of our archetypal great shaykh will later be described as having been attended by signs and miracles, a strange light in the sky, perhaps, or dreams or visions experienced by his mother while carrying him in her womb. The child in question will be recognized as special soon after his birth: quiet and well-behaved, completing the first stage of traditional Islamic education (the learning by heart of the entire text of the Quran) at an astonishingly early age—five, perhaps. Since the child's parents are often a family with local religious responsibilities—the father a village preacher, perhaps, with an uncle who occupies some minor religious or administrative position in a local town—the child's early education will often be in the hands of his family. Having learned the Quran and literacy at home, then, and having spent some time studying the *hadith* traditions of the Prophet with his uncle, the young man will proceed to a local center for further study. Each Muslim country has such a local center, and if it is not one of those pre-eminent in the Muslim world (such as the Azhar in Cairo), our young scholar may leave his home country for a greater city: Cairo, Baghdad, or Damascus. At some point in his early education away from home, the young scholar will have 'taken' a Sufi order, but will soon have realized that his first shaykh can only take him so far. The first shaykh, recognizing the abilities and promise of his follower, will then send him to a greater shaykh of whom he has heard, possibly in yet another country.

The young Sufi will continue traveling, then, and may spend some time with various shaykhs and at a variety of institutions of learning, and often make the pilgrimage to Mecca before he finally meets the shaykh who is destined to guide him. This meeting is a great event, usually attended by some wonder. The young Sufi may, for example, travel to a far and remote place in search of a certain shaykh and ask for him without success, until he finally gives up his search. At this point a man whom he has never seen before, but whom he immediately knows must be the shaykh he has been searching for, will approach him in the street, address him by name, and tell him that his coming was announced in a dream. The young Sufi will feel great love for the shaykh he has at last found, and the shaykh will take the young Sufi to his home or to the order's *zawiya*, showing him extraordinary marks of respect which astonish the shaykh's other followers.

Typically, our young Sufi's new shaykh will have only a few followers, but devoted and very serious ones. He will be old, and after five or ten years during which our Sufi devotes himself to him, the shaykh will die. Before he dies, the shaykh will have authorized our Sufi to pass on the order which he had himself admitted him to, or 'given' him. Our Sufi may also have a similar authorization given to him in a dream or vision by the Prophet, often in the presence or through the intermediary of Khadir, a figure in the Quran whose exact status (man or angel) is unclear, but who appears there as a supremely wise being who briefly trained the young prophet Moses.

Our Sufi will now leave his adopted home and begin to travel again, perhaps to Mecca. After spending a year there, he will set off for his distant home, stopping at various places on the way to teach. In one of these places he will stay longer than usual, and the number of his followers will become so great that he settles there. His followers will build him a house and a *zawiya* for themselves, and our Sufi will marry a local woman and have children. At this point, he has become a shaykh himself, the title in this case being one conferred by general recognition.

Our shaykh may have followers in places other than the town in which he has finally settled. Those who took the order from him in the various places where he stopped to teach on his journey from Mecca remain his followers. As his fame spreads, other young Sufis will come to him from afar, just as he himself once traveled in search of his shaykh. Some of those who come to him will 'take' the order from him, and after spending a few months or years with him return to their own homes. Before they leave, they may be authorized to 'give' their shaykh's order, and on their arrival in their place of origin they may themselves attract a group of followers, loyal to our shaykh though never meeting him.

Eventually, our shaykh will die and will be buried by large numbers of disconsolate mourners—not only his own followers, but also the townspeople, who will have by then come to appreciate that a great *wali* has been living in their midst, perhaps as a result of the *karama* miracles he performs, stories of which they cannot but have heard. Some years later our shaykh's tomb may become somewhat elaborate, and perhaps a mosque will be built over or next to it. The mosque and tomb will then become a place of pilgrimage for those who were never able to visit our shaykh in his lifetime.

The order that our shaykh gave to his followers in his lifetime was that which he had himself 'taken' from his shaykh, and it was referred to by the same name. Increasingly, however, the order 'given' by our shaykh's successor will be referred to by the name of our shaykh, and as the memory of our shaykh's own shaykh fades—as it will, since that shaykh died in a distant country to which no one from the locality has ever been—the origin of the new order will be remembered only in the names listed in the *silsila*. Our shaykh may also have modified the practices he inherited in various ways: an extra element may have been added to the *wird*, perhaps on the instructions of the Prophet appearing to him in a dream. *Khalwa* may have been de-emphasized in response to the difficult conditions of the time. Beyond this, the practice of the new order will anyhow change slowly in many ways over the years, until the new order has become visibly different from that which was its origin. A new and distinct order, then, has come into being. It has its own *wird*, its own practices, and various hagiographical accounts of the life of our shaykh and

54

of his miracles, some in verse and some in prose, which will be recited for centuries on occasions such as the *mawlid* now celebrated at his tomb.

The role of Sufism in the spread of Islam

The archetypal biography given above is of a shaykh who is born and dies within the lands of Islam. Many shaykhs, however, travel or traveled beyond the Islamic world of their time, in Southeast Asia, Africa, or, today, the West. Those who 'take' their order in these places become not only Sufis, then, but also converts to Islam.

The origins of the spread of Islam in many regions are hard to establish with certainty, partly because recorded history will often start with the arrival of Islam. The regions which became Muslim in the early centuries of Islam, during the new religion's astonishing wave of expansion and conquest, already had sophisticated and literate cultures. The course of the Islamization of Egypt, Syria, and Persia is thus reasonably well known. This was not the case for areas such as Indonesia, Malaya, and the Sudan, to take three examples of areas which became Muslim without military intervention. The Sudan first emerges into history in state documents referring to rulers with Muslim names, but whose kingdoms do not sound—from rare and scanty mentions in the accounts of travelers—to have been particularly Islamic. In Malaya and Indonesia, early records also suggest nominally Muslim kingdoms with populations which may or may not have been Muslim. This can be explained in terms of rulers taking on the trappings, if not the realities, of apparently more advanced—and certainly more powerful—local cultures. It is not the same as Islamization.

The spread of Islam in Southeast Asia may have been associated with the influence of Muslim traders or with the activities of Sufis. These are in a sense not really alternative explanations, since traders were often Sufis and Sufis were often traders (the use of trade networks to enhance the cohesion of a Sufi community has been noted above). Trade may also provide the material means to support religious activity. It is not clear what the spread of Islam in the Sudan should be associated with, but it is clear that the spread there of knowledge of Islam and of compliance with Islamic norms was the work of Sufis. The picture becomes clearer in the nineteenth and twentieth centuries once there is more information, when a variety of orders can be seen establishing themselves in new areas of the Sudan, East Africa, Somalia, Nigeria, and so on. Usually a shaykh returns from his studies abroad having 'taken' an order which he then 'gives' at home. His followers not only build a house for him and a *zawiya* for themselves, but also a school, and often begin to farm local land, providing an alternative source of economic support to trade. The Sufi-run school is probably the only available educational institution anywhere nearby, and as children go to the school to study they also learn what Islam (rather than local custom) really requires of them and also join their teacher's Sufi order. It is hard to find a Sudanese Muslim who does not have at least a family connection with a Sufi order.

The shaykh who spreads his order outside the lands of Islam, then, is both a standard figure and an important agent of Islamization.

The organization of an order

In its early years, a new Sufi order such as that established by our archetypal shaykh has little formal organization, although our shaykh was represented in distant areas by Sufis who had spent time with him before returning home with his authorization to 'give' the order in their turn. This role is the basis of any order's organization.

Persons who represent a shaykh in this way are called by different names in different orders. In some cases the word used is *khalifa* ('caliph' or 'vicar' or 'representative'), and in some others the term is *madhun* ('authorized one'). These two terms emphasize two different but complimentary functions, representation and authorization. Nearly all shaykhs with more than a dozen followers have some sort of authorized representative, usually looking after followers in areas far from the shaykh's main residence and sometimes acting as an assistant to the shaykh.

Some orders, especially in the nineteenth and twentieth centuries, have much more complex organizational structures than this. One Sudanese order, for example, had an almost military command structure, with several layers of official ranks supervising Sufis of the rank below. Another order in the Sahara separated the spiritual from the administrative control of its many *zawiya*s, which were trading posts and agricultural settlements as well as schools and spiritual centers: regulations specified matters as detailed as how much meat the spiritual director's wife was entitled to eat on which days of the week. An order in Egypt kept membership records as precise as those of a political party, and so on.

In recent centuries, government regulation has forced certain organizational characteristics on many orders. The country with the most elaborate official regulation of Sufism today is Egypt, where Sufism was one of many areas of life affected by the nineteenth-century project of building a modern, centralized state (discussed in Chapter Five). A government appointee was given authority to oversee the orders, and a variety of laws were passed to control their administration and to some extent even their practices. All orders were obliged to register and to keep records of a specified variety in a specified format. The authorities—or rather a Supreme Council for Sufi Affairs—sometimes intervened in the selection of a new shaykh or even replaced one shaykh with another. As a result of this, particularly in Egypt but also in other countries, some orders became more or less bureaucratized, while others simply failed to register, thus depriving themselves of the possibility of public *dhikr* or processions during *mawlids*, but preserving their independence. The full story of the difficulties Sufis have experienced at the hands of modern states is told in Chapter Five. What is significant here is that in some cases it has changed the nature of the organization of the orders in a way which Sufis themselves would not have chosen.

Such complex organizational structures and techniques are however the exception rather than the rule. Most orders have only a loose system of authorized representatives (whom we will call *khalifa*s) reporting personally to the shaykh. The precise role of a *khalifa*, like his title, varies from order to order, but in general he acts as a minor or junior shaykh. He usually holds *dhikr* sessions, teaches, accepts new Sufis into the order, and deals with the day-to-day problems of the community he heads. Some difficulties and questions, particularly those of newer arrivals, will be fully within his experience and competence; those which are not he will refer to the shaykh. The shaykh knows that someone he trusts is keeping an eye on things; the ordinary Sufi has immediate access to someone he knows reasonably well and who will have more time to spend with him than the shaykh himself. A *khalifa* differs from a shaykh in that he can be a more ordinary person: he does not need to be a *wali* or even like a *wali*, since the Sufi's love is not for the *khalifa* but for the shaykh he represents. In the shaykh, the *khalifa* has someone on whom he can rely when in difficulty, and he will normally teach what he has learned from the shaykh. To be a *khalifa* is in a sense an apprenticeship for being a shaykh: nearly all shaykhs were someone's *khalifa* at some point before becoming shaykhs themselves. Most *khalifa*s, though, do not become shaykhs.

Central control of a sort is often exercised in the first generation of an order's existence, but soon fades. If a shaykh in Mecca has a *khalifa* in Malaysia who dies, a replacement will often be selected locally. He may be less inclined to follow the shaykh in Mecca and still less inclined to follow the Meccan shaykh's successor, whom he may never have even met. After a further generation or two, the Meccan and Malaysian branches of the order in question will be aware of each other and may keep up some sort of friendly and mutually respectful relations, but organizationally they will be entirely separate. A similar split may occur to either or both of these now independent branches a generation or so later. Sometimes a newly independent branch will retain its original name; sometimes an adjective will be added to the original name to indicate the locality of the branch; sometimes a branch may acquire a name of its own, in which case it appears as a new order altogether. Some shaykhs resist splits such as these, and some observers have seen them as constituting some sort of setback for an order; but if one remembers the primary objective of a Sufi order, it will be seen that a split is not so terrible. An order exists to provide a context for the practice of Sufism, as a community and for purposes such as *dhikr*. For an individual Sufi, the shaykh matters more than the order, and distant branches of his order are of little immediate relevance. The splitting of an order, then, is less a problem than a means of spreading, rather as when the pod of a flower opens and gives forth seed.

Bodies such as the Supreme Council for Sufi Affairs in Egypt have been particularly active in intervening in succession disputes. Given the role and importance of the shaykh, as noted in the previous chapter, it is clear that the death of a shaykh leaves an immense hole in the lives of those who have followed him, as well as in the order itself. If the order is not to vanish immediately—which happens very rarely indeed—a new shaykh, a successor, has to be found, and this is rarely an easy process. A shaykh may nominate his successor, but this is rare (the Prophet himself did not nominate a successor). Equally, one of the late shaykh's *khalifa*s is sometimes so obviously well qualified to succeed him that no doubt arises. More frequently, however, there are either multiple candidates or no candidate at all. In the case of multiple candidacies, an order may sometimes split into two. This split is not always permanent, since followers from one camp may gradually cross into the other until one of the two new shaykhs is very clearly the main or true successor. When this does not happen, two branches of the order may continue independently; this is especially easy if they are located in a large city, and less easy (and so less likely) in a small village. As has been said, though, it really matters little for the spiritual practice of ordinary Sufis whether an order splits or not.

Where there is no obvious candidate, the succession will often pass to a son of the late shaykh, or occasionally to a daughter, or to a daughter's husband. Hereditary succession of this sort becomes established in most orders sooner or later, giving rise to dynasties of shaykhs, in some areas called 'holy families' by outside observers. There are obvious practical advantages to such a system. Disputes are avoided or run their course quietly within one family. The *zawiya* of an order may be the same as the house of the late shaykh, whose tomb will also be a concern of the order; the ownership of the house and the family tomb thus remain in the hands of the order's shaykh. For these reasons, Egyptian law assumes that the leadership of an order passes in the family, just as property does.

There are also disadvantages to the system. Most obviously, there is no guarantee that wisdom, piety, and sanctity will be inherited. It may be expected that a shaykh's son will have benefitted from the *baraka* enjoyed by all who were in the shaykh's presence, and also that he will have been exposed to the shaykh's influence and training as much as or more than anyone else; this, however, is far from an absolute guarantee. The sons of shaykhs sometimes have interests and inclinations very different from their fathers (as all sons do). Even if a son can play the role of shaykh adequately for many of those followers who remember his father, he may not be able to impress or attract others purely on the basis of his own nature and abilities. In this case, the membership of an order will gradually decline and may even become extinct. Some shaykhs, however, have many sons, and in some cases nephews are also considered eligible to succeed. The larger the field from which a choice may be made, the greater the chances of a suitable new shaykh being found; there is an observable correlation between the number of a shaykh's offspring and the future health and growth of his order.

Two solutions are possible when the son of a shaykh succeeds, but proves inadequate to his task. One is that another follower of the late shaykh fulfills the more difficult spiritual tasks incumbent on a shaykh, leaving the new shaykh with largely ceremonial roles, such as leading the *dhikr*. The other is that older followers join a different, related shaykh in some collateral branch of his order: earlier splits can thus guarantee the longevity of an order, just as genetic diversity does in the case of living beings. Whether a Sufi remains with his original branch, or finds another branch or even another order, depends largely on his own spiritual aspirations. Those Sufis who are to travel to the highest reaches of the path usually pass through the hands of a number of shaykhs anyhow, as we have noted, while a minor shaykh whose actions are conditioned largely by the tradition within which he operates will often suffice for those whose involvement in Sufism is less deep.

Some of the great orders and their shaykhs

A Sufi order is, in its origin, a shaykh and his followers. The orders established by the very earliest shaykhs were not usually given names and are thus generally invisible to later historians; the practice of naming orders after certain shaykhs is first found in the late twelfth century (around the time of al-Ghazali and Ibn al-'Arabi), when a number of orders which are still in existence today emerged from the teachings of their eponymous shaykhs. Among these were the Qadiriya, named after 'Abd al-Qadir al-Jilani (1078–1166), and the Rifa'iya, named after Ahmad al-Rifa'i (1106–82). The thirteenth century saw the emergence of the Shadhiliya, named after Abu al-Hasan al-Shadhili (1187–1258), and the Mevleviya, named after Mevlana Jalal al-Din Rumi (d. 1273). In the fourteenth century, the Naqshbandiya arose, named after Baha al-Din Naqshband (1318–89). These orders emerged in various places across the Islamic world. 'Abd al-Qadir al-Jilani was born in Persia and taught in Baghdad, as did Ahmad al-Rifa'i; al-Shadhili was a Moroccan who lived in Spain, taught in Tunis, and settled in Alexandria, while Rumi was born in Afghanistan and taught in Turkey. Naqshband, on the other hand, was born and taught in the same place: Bukhara, now in Uzbekistan. All these orders spread far beyond their places of origin, though not always evenly.

New orders continued to emerge after the fourteenth century, sometimes as offshoots of earlier orders with slightly different names or sometimes with the same name: that an order
in Egypt in 1650 and in Malaysia in 1950 are both called
'Shadhiliya' does not mean that they are the same thing. The
difference between individual branches of an old-established
order may sometimes be as great as the differences between
that order as a whole and other orders. Nomenclature, then,
is not so important and is often misleading.

Entirely new orders also continued to come into being, especially in the eighteenth and nineteenth centuries, which saw the
birth of orders such as the Tijaniya, from Ahmad al-Tijani
(1745–1815), and the Ahmadiya, from Ahmad ibn Idris
(1760–1837). The twentieth century, too, has seen new orders,
but not generally of the same significance: most twentieth-
century orders remain, so far, limited to their countries of origin.

We will now consider in slightly more detail the histories
of three of these orders. The first two have been selected as
representative of the half-dozen or so great and ancient orders;
the third has been selected as a representative of the more
recent orders and also because it happens to be an order
which has been well studied by various scholars, and so one
about which more is known than is the case with most others.

The Qadiriya

'Abd al-Qadir al-Jilani was born in Persia in 1078. He died
in 1166 in Baghdad, where he had been a shaykh since 1127.
He moved to Baghdad to study and specialized in the
Hanbali school of legal interpretation; his first shaykh was
probably one Hamad al-Dabbas, but he later received his
order from Khadir (for whom see above). Little else is known
of 'Abd al-Qadir's life with much certainty, though his sober
orthodoxy was always much stressed.

The order named after him spread far and fast, in his lifetime to the Yemen and Syria, and shortly after his death to the Hijaz, Turkestan, Egypt, and Morocco, from where it passed, with Islam itself, south to Senegal. By the fifteenth century it was established in Turkey, and at the same time it spread to India. The sixteenth century saw its arrival in the Sudan, the seventeenth in China and Malaysia, and the eighteenth in Greece, Bosnia, and Albania. In the nineteenth century it was established in Somalia, whence it spread in the early twentieth century to Zanzibar and other areas of East Africa. In the twentieth century it appeared for the first time in Siberia, carried there by Stalin's deportees from the Caucasus.

This picture of continuous outward spread is somewhat misleading, however. The Qadiriya, like any Sufi order, may be present at a particular place *in* a country, not throughout a country: we are talking about one or more shaykhs or *khalifa*s in one or more towns, not about nation-wide coverage. We are also talking about decay as well as growth. In the fourteenth century the most important Syrian center of the Qadiriya was in the city of Hama, while in the sixteenth century Aleppo had replaced Hama. The history of the Qadiriya is not a unitary one; it is the sum of the histories of a number of individual shaykhs operating in a variety of different circumstances. All that the various branches of the order really have in common, in fact, is a form of liturgy—the *wird*, various prayers, and a form of *dhikr* probably deriving from 'Abd al-Qadir himself—and a devotion to the person of 'Abd al-Qadir and some of the other early shaykhs of the order, whose hagiographies are much read and who serve as a source of inspiration for later Qadiris.

The Shadhiliya

The Shadhiliya is almost the contemporary of the Qadiriya. It is named after Abu al-Hasan al-Shadhili (1187–1258) a Moroccan

shaykh from Seville. After studying locally, al-Shadhili traveled
to Baghdad and then back to Morocco, where he took as his
shaykh another Moroccan, 'Abd al-Salam ibn Mashish (d.
1225), the author of an enduringly popular prayer. Like 'Abd al-
Qadir, he was in non-physical communication with Khadir, from
whom he received part of what was to become the Shadhiliya's
liturgy. He then taught in Tunis for some time and finally moved
to Egypt, where he died in 1258 on his way to Mecca for the *hajj*
pilgrimage.

Again, little more than this is known about him. The spread
of the order across the Islamic world could be chronicled as we
have chronicled that of the Qadiriya, but this would serve little
purpose; the history of the Shadhiliya, again, is the sum of the
histories of individual shaykhs. We will, therefore, consider
briefly two of these shaykhs, one early and one late.

The best-known early Shadhili shaykh is Ibn 'Ata Allah of
Alexandria, the city where al-Shadhili spent his most influential years. Ibn 'Ata Allah was born in the mid-thirteenth
century to a family of academic and practicing lawyers.
Although his father had followed al-Shadhili, Ibn 'Ata Allah
himself had no particular interest in Sufism until he met Abu
al-'Abbas al-Mursi (d. 1287), the successor of al-Shadhili.
On meeting him, he immediately found that he loved him. He
continued his legal studies, becoming a senior professor at
the prestigious Azhar university in Cairo, where he died in
1309, having also become the third shaykh of the Shadhiliya
after the death of his own shaykh. He is universally known
among Sufis for his collection of *Hikam* (sayings), a selection
of which are given at the end of this book. The manuscript of
these was made by a follower of Ibn 'Ata Allah's, Taqi al-Din
al-Subki (–1355), also later a famous shaykh. Many Sufi texts
originate in this way, as notes made by a student rather than
the written composition of the author himself. This reflects

65

the extent to which Sufi teaching is by its nature oral; any written text can only give a part of the message in a generalized form. The *Hikam*, however, gives as good a taste of what it is like to sit at the feet of a great shaykh as can any merely written work.

A well-known recent Shadhili shaykh is Abu Hamid al-'Arabi al-Darqawi (1760–1823), origin of the Darqawiya, an order in its own right which is also described as a Shadhili order in recognition of its origins. Among his students was Muhammad al-Madani (1780–1847), from Medina. At the age of twenty-seven al-Madani left the Hijaz for Morocco, where he visited various shaykhs, finally staying with al-Darqawi in Fez. After al-Darqawi's death, al-Madani proceeded independently and attracted many followers in the Hijaz, Algeria, Tunisia, and especially in western Libya. It was in the Tripolitanian coastal town of Misrata that Nur al-Din 'Ali al-Yashruti (d. 1899) met and took from al-Madani, thereafter staying with him until his shaykh's death. Al-Madani was succeeded by his son, Muhammad Zafir (1828–1903), the shaykh of the future Ottoman sultan, 'Abd al-Hamid. Muhammad Zafir spent the years 1876–1906 in Istanbul, residing at a *zawiya* which the sultan had constructed for him near the Yildiz palace.

Al-Yashruti, however, left the Madaniya (as the followers of al-Madani were often known) and traveled east with nine followers, finally arriving at Acre in Palestine, where he established a *zawiya* of his own, attracting progressively more followers and, from the 1860s, acting no longer in the name of the Darqawiya but in the name of his own Yashrutiya—a further split. The Yashrutiya was led after his death by his own sons, and his daughter Fatima wrote a number of texts for the order. The Yashrutiya survives to this day, though the creation of the State of Israel, into which Acre has been incorporated, led to the transfer of the *zawiya* to Amman (Jordan).

The Ahmadiya

Our third order, the Ahmadiya, is named after Ahmad ibn Idris (1760–1837), a Moroccan scholar who started to teach in Mecca in 1799. It has nothing to do with the Pakistani-originating heterodox movement of the same name. Before arriving in Mecca, Ibn Idris studied various aspects of Islam in his country of origin, had 'taken' orders from a number of shaykhs there, and had also been in contact with the Tariqa Muhammadiya. This was a movement which in general emphasized man's direct (rather than mediated) relationship with God and the Sufi's direct connection with the Prophet. It inspired a number of new Sufi orders during the eighteenth century, of which the Ahmadiya was the last. Like many other great shaykhs, Ibn Idris received the command to establish his own following directly from the Prophet, in the non-physical presence of Khadir.

Ibn Idris gathered around him in Mecca a small number of devoted followers. These addressed him not as 'shaykh,' but as *ustadh*, professor, and he referred to them not as followers but as students. He taught them the intricacies of the basic texts of Islam, the Quran and the *hadith*, and largely ignored the work of academic scholars, the *ulema*. He stressed that piety and divine inspiration were the most important qualifications for settling disputed questions of law and practice, far more important than the precedent beloved of the *ulema*. He also taught them prayers, some of which he had received from the Prophet and some of his own composition, and trained them to achieve a constant spiritual awareness of the Prophet, an awareness so close that it was a form of contact.

As a result of political disputes in Mecca in which, as a prominent resident, he could hardly have avoided becoming involved, Ibn Idris was obliged to leave Mecca. During his

time there Mecca was twice captured by foreign armies, and
the dynasty of a ruler who had patronized Ibn Idris was
replaced by its enemies. On leaving Mecca, Ibn Idris traveled
south to the remote Yemeni town of Sabya, accompanied by
most of his companions. Here he continued teaching until his
death. On leaving Mecca, Ibn Idris had appointed
Muhammad ibn al-Sanusi (1787–1859) to lead those of his
followers who remained there. Al-Sanusi, also from the Arab
West, had joined Ibn Idris late in life, after becoming an
established scholar and Sufi in his own right: that a senior
shaykh should himself take a shaykh at the point in his
career where one would expect him to be taking followers
rather than new teachers is eloquent testimony to the power
of Ibn Idris's teachings, personality, and *baraka*. By his own
account, al-Sanusi was instructed to follow Ibn Idris by the
Prophet in a dream. After Ibn Idris's death, al-Sanusi became
a leading shaykh himself, with a following not only in the area
around Mecca, but also across the Sahara, especially in what
was later to become Libya. He established a network of
zawiyas, in which most aspects of the life of his followers
were regulated by more than usually detailed rules (including
the one about the meat entitlement of the shaykh's wife). Most
of these followers were uneducated nomads, and as well as
training them in Islam and in Sufism, his order worked for
their general education and improvement. Al-Sanusi himself,
however, remained the scholar he had been before, returning
whenever possible from the desert to Mecca and his library
there. After his death his order was administered by his
descendants, spreading most importantly to Indonesia. It
later became known as the Sanusiya (except in Indonesia,
where it continued to be known as the Ahmadiya).

Al-Sanusi was not the only follower of Ibn Idris who became
a shaykh in his own right. Even before Ibn Idris's death, a Hijazi

of Indian origin, Muhammad 'Uthman al-Mirghani (1793–1852) had established a following across the Red Sea in the Sudan. Whereas al-Sanusi had joined Ibn Idris as a mature man, al-Mirghani joined him at the tender age of fifteen and was still comparatively young when he first left for the Sudan, in 1815, to spread his order there. Although deriving considerable prestige from his connection with Ibn Idris in Mecca, the order that al-Mirghani spread was not exactly that of his own shaykh. Containing elements of the practice and teachings of a number of other orders, it soon described itself as the Khatmiya (a name derived from the word *khatm*, meaning 'seal' or definitive conclusion). Al-Mirghani asserted that his own order was the *khatm* of all the orders, superseding and comprehending them all. He attracted many followers, some individuals and also some minor local shaykhs, whose own followers thus became followers of the Khatmiya and of al-Mirghani personally. After his death, the Khatmiya was spread to Somalia by his nephew, who was half Somali.

Both al-Sanusi and al-Mirghani made modifications to the order they had received: in both cases in organization, and in one case in doctrine and practice. Ibn Idris was evidently aware of some of al-Mirghani's activities in the Sudan, but seems to have been mostly concerned by the extent to which al-Mirghani's own spiritual development might be suffering from "the adulation of crowds." He was not aware of al-Sanusi's organizational innovations, since these happened after his death, but might not have disapproved, since al-Sanusi's objective—the improvement of the Bedouin—had also been an objective of the Tariqa Muhammadiya movement from the beginning.

A further follower of Ibn Idris who later acquired a significant following of his own was Ibrahim al-Rashid (1813–74), a Sudanese. Al-Rashid made no modifications, either doctrinal or organizational, to the Ahmadiya, and remained based in Mecca, as Ibn Idris had himself originally been. Mecca was at this time a great center for Sufism and, of course, a great center for Muslims from all over the Islamic world because of the annual *hajj* pilgrimage. Many visitors to the Hijaz took the Ahmadiya from al-Rashid and then established it in their places of origin on their return; it spread in this way to Malaysia, for example. Two followers of al-Rashid were particularly important in spreading the Ahmadiya further. One took it to India, Turkey, and parts of the Levant. Another, an Egyptian, Muhammad al-Dandarawi (1839–1911), took it down the coast of East Africa. He also established a large following of his own in many areas where Ahmadis already existed, including Egypt, Syria, and Malaya. Of these, Malaya later became a Dandarawi-Ahmadi center in its own right: from Malaya the Ahmadiya spread to Cambodia, Thailand, and Singapore. In turn, from a shaykh in Singapore, 'Abd al-Rashid ibn Muhammad Said (1918–92), it passed to Brunei and also to Italy, from where a very small following in Paris derives.

The speed at which the Ahmadiya spread, and the proximity of these events to our own time, makes it possible to ask how much the Ahmadiya at the end of the twentieth century in Paris or Cairo or Bangkok or Beirut resembles the followers of Ahmad ibn Idris in Mecca two centuries before. The answer to this question is: not very much. The same prayers are used (with some modifications). Ahmad ibn Idris himself is universally respected and to some extent venerated. Most of Ibn Idris's distinctive teaching has, however, vanished without a trace. In its place are various characteristics related to the order's area of destination, rather than of origin. In Italy one finds Traditionalism, a school of thought of French origin (to be discussed below). In Cairo and Beirut one finds an attempt to

70

create a 'third way' between Sufism and Salafism (to be discussed in Chapter Five). In the Central Plains of Thailand, one finds that Sufism has almost vanished and that the main *zawiya* has become a village mosque combined with a state-run primary school where most of the teachers are now Buddhists. In some corners the original Ahmadiya still exists, but these survivals are few, small, and atypical.

The Ahmadiya, then, lost its specificity as it spread, as do all other orders, to a greater or lesser extent. It is hard to be different. It is harder still to maintain difference as the generation of those who enthusiastically followed a newly arrived great shaykh is succeeded by later generations, often the children or grandchildren of the first followers, sometimes following the child or grandchild of the first shaykh. The general features of Sufism common to all the orders are often adopted, and in the end the difference between one order and another is not so great. Differences of litany and hagiography remain, but Ahmadis from the branch of al-Sanusi and Ahmadis from the branch of al-Rashid resemble one another in most other respects. For that matter, they differ little from Qadiris or Shadhilis: Sufis are, in the main, Sufis.

Sufism in the West today

As has been seen, in the centuries after Islam's initial explosion across the Arab world through Persia and beyond, Sufism was an important vehicle for the spread of Islam. Sufis have always been found in countries where the religion of the majority is not Islam, and this is as true today of the West as it is of countries like Thailand and Singapore. Sufi orders are present in France and the United States, in Denmark and Italy; Sufi works are written in or translated into English and French as well as Arabic and Persian.

71

Some of the Sufi orders in the West do not differ in any important respect from their counterparts in the Islamic world or in non-Muslim countries outside the West. A Senegalese immigrant worker in Italy, for example, may belong to an Italian branch of the same order to which his brother belongs in Senegal. Indeed, one Senegalese order has been particularly active among expatriate Senegalese in Italy, providing them not only with spiritual guidance but also with material assistance. Senegalese *khalifa*s travel to Italy much as they might travel to a distant part of Senegal. Much the same thing happens with Muslim immigrants in other countries.

The shaykhs and *khalifa*s of such orders in Western countries do, of course, have to cope with problems that do not occur elsewhere. In the first place, most countries' emigrants to the West are not a cross-section of their own country's society, but tend rather to be from among those groups who are unlearned in Islam. This is because they are usually either from the poorest sections of society with no education at all (in which case they emigrated because they saw no future at home) or are people who were educated in Western technical and scientific disciplines, emigrating because they see a brighter future in the West. In neither case will emigrants have had much education in Islam. Secondly and most importantly, cultural and social conditions in the West are far from ideal for the practice of Islam or of Sufism. Many Western social practices contradict Islamic and Sufi values and practices, and Western culture for various reasons has more influence over Muslim minorities in the West than has the local culture on Muslim minorities in many other parts of the world. Despite these problems, however, the differences between first-generation immigrants' Sufi orders in the West and the Sufi orders we have so far been considering, are not important.

At the other extreme, there are certain so-called Sufi groups in the West which have more to do with the West than with Islam or with the Sufism which this book describes. Their origin is not the movement of Muslims or of Islam toward the West, but rather the search of Westerners for sources of religious truth and comfort from outside the Christian churches. This search is in some senses a part of Western modernity, particularly since the age of the French Revolution, and since the start of the nineteenth century Westerners have often found material and inspiration in non-Western religions, especially in Hinduism and Buddhism. Various nineteenth-century groups, of which the most important was Madame Blavatsky's Theosophical Society, made use of Hindu or Buddhist teachings, texts, and concepts, out of which they created something distinctively new and different. By the end of the twentieth century, many religious concepts of non-Western origin had become part of Western civilization as a whole. The (originally Hindu) concepts of *karma* and reincarnation, for example, are now known to almost everyone, if rarely understood in quite the same way as they are in their cultures and religions of origin.

Non-Christian monotheistic religions have provided the West with less material than Hinduism and Buddhism: both Judaism and Islam seem to have been of too solid and too rigid a construction to be adopted piecemeal. Sufism, the most flexible aspect of Islam, has, however, been mined with some success, as has the Kabbala, the Jewish mystical tradition. Western borrowings from Sufism did not follow quite the same pattern as from Hinduism. The two most important sources of Westernized Sufism were Muslim by birth (though one had a Scottish mother), not Westerners like Madame Blavatsky of the Theosophical Society. The first of these was an Indian, Inayat Khan, who published his *Sufi Message of*

73

Spiritual Liberty in England in 1914. The second was Idries Shah, who published *The Sufis* in 1964. Books by both men remain very popular today, but would be seen by the vast majority of Sufis in the Islamic world as teaching something other than Sufism, if only because they present Sufism as something which can be separated from Islam. As has been seen, Sufism is a path within Islam, and so can only become something very different if removed from that context.

Idries Shah and Inayat Khan were themselves both Muslim by birth, but their followers were generally non-Muslim Westerners for whom Sufism was not an aspect of Islam but something self-contained, sometimes something closer to a philosophy of life than a religious practice. For many such non-Muslim Western Sufis, Sufism is not only something separate (or at least separable) from Islam, but also something to be mixed with other religions and practices. Sociologists have pointed out that for some searchers after religious truth, searching may become a habit. In a sense, the search for truth becomes an obstacle to finding it, since even when such 'searchers' find something (such as Sufism) they do not stop to immerse themselves in and practice what they have found. Instead, they often continue their search, as did one of Inayat Khan's most important American followers, Samuel Lewis. Lewis took various 'regular' orders (such as the Naqshbandiya and Shadhiliya) in the Islamic world, but mixed Zen Buddhism and Hinduism with his Sufism. Three years before his death in 1971, he was ordained by a Korean Zen teacher in the United States. This sort of syncretism is typical of many neo-Sufi groups found in the West. It is very different from the non-Western Sufism we have so far been examining.

Somewhere between these neo-Sufi religious movements and the standard Sufi orders of Muslim immigrants to the

West lie what may be called Western Sufi orders. One of the most important of these is a branch of the Naqshbandiya led by a Turkish Cypriot shaykh, Muhammad Nazim al-Qubrusi. Since he grew up in what was then part of the British Empire, Muhammad Nazim learned rather better English at school than do most shaykhs. After an early career similar to that of our archetypal shaykh (considered in Chapter Three), Nazim succeeded his own shaykh in Damascus. As well as concerning himself with his followers in Syria, Lebanon, and his native Cyprus, however, in 1974 Shaykh Nazim made his first visit to England. Twenty years later, in the late 1990s, more than three thousand people a night attended the London mosque (in the suburb of Peckham) where he led prayers during Ramadan. By this time he also had sizeable followings in Germany and the United States, as well as in the Islamic world from the Levant to the Far East. Every year he visited his followers in four different continents, spending relatively little time at his home in the Turkish Republic of Northern Cyprus.

Although Shaykh Nazim's followers in the Islamic world differ little from Sufis following other orders there, his followers in the West are different from the followers of the immigrant orders we considered earlier. Those among them who were born Muslim (Turkish, Arab, Pakistani, and Malay immigrants of the first or second generation) are following what is for them a new order, not one from within their ethnic communities. More importantly, many of Nazim's followers are ethnic European or American converts to Islam, the majority of whom he was instrumental in bringing to Islam. Though converts, these are indisputably Muslim in a way that most of the followers of teachers such as Idries Shah and Inayat Khan are not. As has been stated before, any order in the West has to cope with problems which are not found else-

75

where, and this is particularly true when dealing with Western converts; but although certain rules may need temporarily to be relaxed because of special circumstances, the practice and conduct of Nazim's Western followers does not differ in any important respect from that of his non-Western followers, or from that of Naqshbandis anywhere.

Nazim's order, then, differs from the immigrant orders in that it has an independent identity in the West and to some extent grew in the West rather than being imported to the West fully grown. It differs from the neo-Sufi groups in that its doctrine and practices are not Westernized in any significant way and in its having large numbers of followers in the Islamic world, not just in the West. It also differs from another group of Western Sufi orders, which may be described as Traditionalist orders.

The Traditionalist orders derive from a special case in the history of Western borrowing from Eastern religions. René Guénon, a French writer on religion, began his career in the *fin-de-siècle* Paris milieu of occultism, Freemasonry, and neo-Hinduism. He became increasingly disenchanted with what he came to see as 'counterfeit' spirituality, finally devoting himself to Islam and Sufism and moving to Egypt, where he joined a Shadhili order. Before his death in 1952, he had become an Egyptian citizen. Guénon's writings portrayed modernity as a dark age and argued that the only salvation lay in following an 'orthodox' religious tradition, from which definition he excluded mainstream Catholicism.

Guénon's writings have since inspired many to find, in tradition, alternatives to modernity. These alternatives are usually religious ones, but have sometimes been political. The political implications of his work were worked out by an Italian, Julius Evola. Evola's rejection of political modernity earned him a following in Nazi Germany, in the Italian

76

extreme right of the 1960s and 1970s, and in the former
Eastern block after the demise of the Soviet Union. Although
important, political Traditionalism is an unusual response to
Guénon's work. Most of his readers have been drawn toward
religious alternatives to modernity: sometimes in Buddhism
or Orthodox Christianity or Freemasonry, but most typically
in Sufism. In the same way that Evola worked out the political implications of Guénon's writings, a Swiss, Frithjof
Schuon, worked out the Sufi implications—but not in books
and pamphlets as Evola had, but in a Sufi order.

Schuon's order, the Maryamiya, and other orders which
broke away from it, are found in many Western countries and
also in some parts of the Islamic world. These Traditionalist
Sufi orders rarely have large numbers of followers, but their
followers are invariably very active in spreading Islam,
Sufism, and a Traditionalist perspective: they translate,
teach, publish, and broadcast. Their connection with Schuon
and Guénon is rarely explicit, partly out of a general reti-
cence which may be inherited from the secretive habits of the
various groups in which the young Guénon participated.
Traditionalists do not consider themselves to be spreading
the views of Guénon, but rather the truth; for them Guénon
explained the truth, but did not in any sense create it.

These Traditionalist orders are far from the other three
varieties of Sufi orders in the West. Unlike immigrant orders,
their followers are almost exclusively Western converts, usually from the intellectual and cultural elite. Where born
Muslims are to be found, invariably they will be highly
Westernized. Traditionalist orders are also far from the neo-
Sufi orders, in that they consider themselves Muslim and
abhor syncretism (although syncretist elements occasionally
creep in). They differ from orders such as Shaykh Nazim's,
because rather than just growing in the West, they came into

77

being in the West and exist largely independently of all other Muslim groups there. Traditionalists also differ from Muslims in the Islamic world in that the influence of Guénon upon their views, understanding, and actions—if not their practice—is very significant. Guénon was not a shaykh, but his work is more important to Traditionalist Sufis than the work of any individual shaykh is to the followers of any other order in the Muslim world. This alone makes them different.

4 Friends, warriors, and merchants

S ufism has, so far, been considered solely as a religious path. In its essence, intention, and purpose, this is what Sufism is, but in practice it can be and has been other things as well. Mention has already been made of Sufis' commercial activities. In addition to economic significance, Sufism has often had, and sometimes still has, military, political, and social significance.

Sufism and jihad

In the first part of the twentieth century, one of the best-known Sufi orders in the West was the Sanusiya, an order which played an important role in French and Italian colonial history. Ironically, it is now becoming clear that it was the French army's attack on the Sanusiya, an attack itself based on faulty intelligence assessments, which initiated that order's long involvement in *jihad* against first French and later Italian forces. The errors of French intelligence of the time can be to some extent excused: even if the Sanusiya was not originally an active political or military opponent of colonization, it later became one without too much difficulty. Many other Sufi orders in other places were also involved in *jihad*.

Mention has already been made in Chapter Three of a
Daghestani shaykh living in Damascus (it was from him that
Nazim al-Qubrusi took the Naqshbandiya order). He had
arrived there at the age of five as one of many Daghestani
refugees from the Russian subjugation of Daghestan (in the
Caucasus), a subjugation against which his own shaykh had
been active, in a long and bitter resistance led by another
Naqshbandi shaykh, Shamil. The nineteenth century saw
Sufi-led resistance against colonization not only in the
Russian Empire, but also in the British Empire: Sufis led
armed men against the British in India and Somalia. As well
as *jihad*s against European colonization, Sufis at times
launched *jihad*s against secularizing governments in their
own countries: against Egyptian rule in the Sudan, against
the secularizing reforms of the Ottoman Empire in the
Yemen, and against those of Kemal Ataturk in Turkey.

These various military actions may at first sight seem hard
to reconcile with our picture of the Sufi occupied with the
'greater *jihad*' against the *nafs*, withdrawn from the world in
which he lives and concentrating on God. The explanation
lies partly outside religion, in the nature and position of many
of the Sufi orders, and partly inside Islam. The 'greater *jihad*'
may be that against the *nafs*, but the 'lesser *jihad*'—armed
struggle—is far from unimportant. Islam was not spread *only*
by the sword, but the sword played a part in its spread. In the
early centuries of Islam, many countries of the Middle East
were 'opened' to Islam (as the Arabic term usually used for
these conquests literally translates) by Muslim armies. These
conquests would never have happened without the *jihad* of
the soldiers serving in these armies, even though there were
often reasons for the local inhabitants to welcome Muslim
rule. In the case of Egypt, Spain, and Cyprus, for example,
there was an expectation that Muslim rulers would discontin-

ue the persecutions of local versions of Christianity which the inhabitants of these areas were then suffering at the hands of Christian rulers. Despite this, the conditions which encouraged gradual and pacific conversion to Islam over the succeeding centuries would not have obtained without *jihad*.

Jihad does not only have its place in the history of Islam, but also in the spiritual practice of Islam. In the West, we have learned to see that many motives other than the pure love of God motivated the Crusaders, and many base motives were surely among those of later Muslim soldiers, too. The archetypal *jihad* in Islam is, however, that of the time of the Prophet, when little immediate advantage was to be gained from fighting. Although the victors in a battle enjoyed plunder (as was the custom of the place and time), the war between the new Muslims under the Prophet and his Meccan adversaries was in the nature of a civil war, dividing families and testing loyalties. Half-hearted commitment to the new religion was most visible on the battlefield, and the Quran and the *hadith* are full of passages relating to commitment to Islam and sacrifice in war. The atmosphere and environment at this time, then, was such that participation in *jihad* was a very real act of subjugation of the *nafs*, of turning to God. This is how *jihad* came to be counted among the religious practices of Islam: to give one's life for something, or to be prepared to give one's life, is seen as the ultimate act of commitment to God and His religion. Islam, then, does call for the 'lesser *jihad*' as well as the 'greater *jihad*.' As devout Muslims, Sufis were and are more inclined to answer that call than many of the less devout, just as they were and are more inclined to scrupulous observance of fasts and prayer times.

Sufi shaykhs and orders were also well positioned to answer the call for *jihad*. A Sufi shaykh often plays a special role in Islamic societies because he is a major figure whose position is

81

independent of almost all other interests and structures. His position depends almost exclusively on his own prestige, or at the least the prestige of the order which he leads, which is also independent of other structures. Shaykhs are therefore frequently called on by those who are not their followers to act as arbitrators. This is particularly true in tribal societies, where an arbitrator must of necessity be outside the tribes in question, as a shaykh (who may have come from a distant corner of the Islamic world) often is. In times of crisis, a Sufi shaykh may similarly be called on to give wider leadership.

The Yemeni *jihad* against the Ottoman Empire at the start of the twentieth century, for example, was led by a young shaykh who had initially worked to pacify warring tribes as a first step toward bringing them closer to God. His success in settling various disputes between tribes derived partly from his status as a respected shaykh (he was a learned man and a possible *wali*, and certainly the descendant of an undoubted *wali*) and partly on his being from outside the tribes in question: his family came from Morocco, his wife from the Sudan. After settling disputes, he was successful in persuading the tribes to live according to Islamic law rather than tribal custom and violence. It was thus an easy step from arbitration to leading the tribes he had pacified against a weak Ottoman force when the decision was made in faraway Istanbul to replace Islamic law with a modern (and for the Yemenis a profoundly alien) civil law. This Yemeni *jihad* was one of the few Sufi *jihad*s to achieve some measure of success. Distant events made first the Italians and then the British eager to support it against the Ottomans, and the shaykh who had led it became the ruler of an internationally recognized state which disappeared only after his death (when it was incorporated into the powerful new kingdom of Saudi Arabia along with other previously independent territories).

The position of the order, as well as that of the shaykh, places Sufis in a position from which *jihad* can easily be launched. An order may be small in absolute numbers, but many cover wide areas: sometimes a region within a country, sometimes more than one country. The members of the order are used to obeying instructions, and this makes them potentially significant organizations for many purposes. In the case of the Sanusi *jihad*, for example, the tribes of Cyrenaica (later in Libya) looked to the Sanusiya for leadership against the Italians partly because the Sanusis had already withstood attack by French forces, but mostly because there was no other existing organization which rose above the level of the tribe. There was simply no other pre-existing organization to co-ordinate resistance.

The political importance of Sufi orders is not restricted to *jihad* or to tribal societies. Even in societies with more developed institutions than those of the Yemen or the Sahara, an order may still become involved in politics. A shaykh may suggest to his followers that they vote for a particular candidate in an election, for example. In some countries, a shaykh who lends his support to the regime in power may reap handsome rewards: official support can help an order to grow or at least to avoid persecution. It is unusual, however, for political involvement to go as far as it did in the Sudan, where one of the two main political parties—the Unionist Party—is the political face of the Khatmiya order and where members of the main family of Sufi shaykhs have thus served as Prime Minister.

In all periods and regions, there are many examples of Sufi involvement in politics. Mostly this involvement is marginal, and the order is affected by it only a little. Sometimes aspects of an order are changed significantly, especially in tightly-controlled states such as Hafez al-Assad's Syria. The rewards of an alliance with the Syrian regime are high, but a price must be paid: an order's teaching is expected to reflect official propaganda. Even in states such as Turkey, too great a concentration on matters political may in effect submerge the Sufi origins of an organization in a new identity. In the Sudan, the Khatmiya order still exists as a Sufi order alongside the Unionist Party, but its political significance means that it can hardly remain a normal order. An extreme case is the shaykh who established his own state in the Yemen. He soon found himself occupied with the matters that normally occupy rulers in turbulent times: international alliances, joint operations with British naval forces during the First World War, problems of revenue and expenditure, and so on. He himself seems to have remained a Sufi shaykh with a few followers, but there was ultimately nothing distinctively Sufi about the state he ruled, to the extent that many outside observers were quite oblivious to the fact that there was any connection with Sufism at all.

Most Sufis do not, however, become involved in politics. The saying that "the best man is he who is not known to the Sultan and knows not the Sultan" has already been referred to, and Sufi literature and proverbs abound with warnings of the corrupting consequences of contact with power. Sufism may sometimes become political, and many shaykhs may have some involvement in politics, but politics is far from Sufism's heart.

Sufism and commerce

Commerce is nearer Sufism's heart than politics, since (as has already been mentioned) commercial activities can reinforce the sense of community of an order. Many orders have thus become heavily involved in economic matters without losing anything of their original identity. The use of a network of Sufis for trade has different implications from the use of the same network to support a political party.

In the absence of the various modern devices such as letters of credit and international banks which make long-distance trade easier and safer, Sufi trade networks were particularly important from an economic point of view. The difficulties of doing business with someone in a distant region can be significantly reduced if some non-commercial connection reduces the risk of default. Family connections have often been used to this end, but there is a natural limit to the size of family networks. Overseas Chinese have used ethnic networks, and ethnic-religious networks have been of use to the Jewish diaspora. Sufi networks are thus just one more example of something found in many regions and periods.

Trade is not, however, the only commercial activity in which Sufis became involved. A certain amount of voluntary, communal labor is found in almost any order, as it is in almost any voluntary organization. At the very least, someone will make tea or cook food; someone may also make available premises for an order to meet in and maintain those premises. Sometimes, Sufis will work together to build their order's *zawiya*; in some parts of the world, they will continue to work together to provide funds for the *zawiya* and for those who use it. In the Sudan, for example, where land is plentiful if poor, it has been common for many centuries for a shaykh to establish on virgin land a *khalwa* (as the Sudanese call it) consisting of a few houses and a mosque. The shaykh's followers then work the surrounding land, keeping some of the produce themselves and using some to support the community, which often comes to include children from the locality, sent to attend school at the *khalwa*. These Sudanese communities sometimes grow to become regular villages, their origins remembered only in the name they continue to bear: the *khalwa* of Shaykh So-and-So. Such Sufi communities are the norm in the Sudan and are found in certain other countries as the creations of particular

85

orders. In Senegal, the Mouride order has a city of its own, Touba. In Somalia, several orders established agricultural settlements in.parts of the country in the nineteenth and twentieth centuries, and the Sanusiya established *zawiyas* across the Sahara. In some other countries, though, such as Egypt and Syria, such communities are unknown.

One reason why self-sufficient Sufi communities are found in some places and not others is purely economic. The more sophisticated a region's economy, the more difficult it is to establish a commune. If land is cheap or even free and most people's everyday needs do not exceed what they can produce, a commune with a standard of living similar to the local norm can be established quite easily.

There is more than this, however, to many Sufi settlements in certain regions. Certain orders have at times occupied themselves with the problem of the Bedouin, particularly (as has been seen) those related to the Tariqa Muhammadiya movement. For many Europeans and for some Arabs, the Bedouin symbolize freedom and nobility; for most Arabs, they have more usually symbolized ignorance and crime—crime because when conditions in the desert are hard, Bedouin tribes raid the edges of settled areas, and because certain tribes have made a practice of attacking and stealing from those who pass through their territories. Even in the early decades of the twentieth century, pilgrims traveling from Mecca to Medina needed a military escort to protect them from Bedouin attack, and pilgrims as well as soldiers were frequently killed. The Bedouin may revere poetry, but were until very recently almost always illiterate and usually knew little of Islam, not just of those parts of Islamic Law which forbade stealing the transport and possessions of pilgrims, but even of those dealing with matters relating to prayer. Even when the Bedouin did know of Islamic Law, tribal custom

in general took precedence. Many Muslims came to the conclusion that the Bedouin needed to be settled in order to
restrain their criminal activities; some also realized that settlement was a prerequisite to remedying Bedouin ignorance in
matters of religion. Settlements were thus established in the
Sahara, parts of the Arabian peninsula, and Somalia to make
Bedouin better Muslims, not just to create Sufi communities.
In these settlements one might see a parallel to the role
(already considered) which the Sufi orders played in the
spread of Islam.

Sufism and sociability

As has been observed, the activities of Sufi orders provide
unusual opportunities for sociability in societies where few
such opportunities exist. Like commerce, sociability may
strengthen the community of the order and so assist in Sufis'
practice. Sometimes, sociability may become the main fea-
ture of an order. This is particularly likely with older orders,
where the position of shaykh has been handed down for several generations within a family. In such cases a new shaykh
may of course turn out to be a *wali* at the level of the first
shaykhs under whom the order came into existence, but this
rarely happens, partly because such a person is more likely
to start a new branch of an order somewhere else than to follow a minor shaykh until his death and then take over. It is
also the case that the longer an order has been established,
the larger the proportion of its followers who belong to it
because their parents did. As has been observed, the degree
of commitment of such people is generally lower, the role
played in their lives by Sufism less important.

In some cases, then, a Sufi order can become more of a
local tradition than anything resembling the dynamic and
often fast-growing groups of Sufis we have considered in con-

texts such as the life of our archetypal shaykh. In cities, such 'social' Sufi orders may blend into each other to produce a sort of general Sufi milieu inhabited by people who may not even follow a particular shaykh, but who attend a variety of *dhikr*s and *mawlid*s, listen to chants and music, meet friends, talk, and drink tea. Even though Sufism has in these cases become more a social than a religious activity, it would be wrong to see it as exclusively social. Many people in Europe go to church because one goes to church, but that does not stop going to church being a religious activity with spiritual consequences.

5 Whose orthodoxy?

As has been remarked, particularly in the nineteenth century, Western scholars frequently placed Sufism in opposition to Islamic orthodoxy. From a purely historical point of view, this is incorrect. Muslims, too, have denied the orthodoxy of Sufism, however, particularly in the twentieth century, but also in earlier periods. Sufis have always had to deal with opposition, perhaps inevitably given their position as a sort of minority within Islam. Minorities everywhere attract opposition, if only because they are different, and differences from any norm tend to produce tension with that norm.

Sufis are perhaps lucky that Islam is in general a tolerant religion. Although in theory the strictest possible penalty—death—is prescribed for a Muslim who turns to disbelief, and although a wide variety of acts and views have been classified as indicators of disbelief, actual executions have been very rare indeed. The systematic persecutions of doctrinal opponents·so familiar in European history are almost unknown. One ingenious response to the existence of difference of opinion within the community of Muslims has been to concede that more than one view may be right. Thus there are seven authoritative readings of the Quran, differing from one another in a number of admittedly very minor ways.

Of all the different schools of legal interpretation which came into being in the early centuries of Islam, four have survived down the centuries; all of these are considered equally correct, even when they differ on important points. Sufism has benefitted from this spirit of general tolerance, of reluctance to create open breaches. There are exceptions, however, and it is with them that this chapter deals.

The three opponents of Sufi practice who are considered below are not the only figures who have condemned Sufis, but are probably the most important. In all three cases, the opposition was not to Sufism as such, but to particular Sufi practices. In all cases, too, opposition to specific Sufi practices was part of an attempt to reform Islam as a whole, an attempt which produced an exception to the general rule of tolerance with regard to many or all other Muslims, not just Sufis.

From Ibn Taymiya to the Wahhabis

The earliest major critic of Sufi practices was Taqi al-Din ibn Taymiya (1263–1328). Ibn Taymiya was a Syrian academic from a well-established scholarly family, a lawyer and theologian. He was also a strict and uncompromising man: his first action on returning home from the pilgrimage he made in 1293, for example, was to write an exposé and condemnation of various unorthodox practices he had noticed while in Mecca. As well as being uncompromising, he was also brave: when in 1299 Damascus was threatened by the Mongols who had already sacked Baghdad, Ibn Taymiya went out to the camp of the allied Mongol and Georgian armies to argue with the Tartar khan, Ghazan. The khan was himself Muslim (unlike his ancestors), and Ibn Taymiya managed to convince him that it was therefore not right for him to sack a Muslim city.

To write to a Sufi shaykh in Cairo, as Ibn Taymiya did in 1305 to condemn the teachings of Ibn al-'Arabi, might seem less foolhardy than to go out to face an invading Mongol, but it had more serious consequences for him personally. The letter was not his first challenge to Sufis—he had already accused the Sufis of one popular order, the Rifa'iya, of counterfeiting miracles—but it was one which was answered. Syria was then under the authority of the Mamluk sultans in Cairo, and the Egyptian Sufi who had received Ibn Taymiya's letter arranged for Ibn Taymiya to be interrogated in Damascus and then summoned to Cairo by the sultan. Ibn Taymiya was imprisoned in Egypt in 1306 and 1308 and again from 1309 to 1313, after which he returned to his teaching in Damascus. In 1318 he was imprisoned again for ignoring an order of the sultan forbidding him to issue *fatwas* (legal opinions) contradicting the decisions of the sultan's council on matters quite unconnected with his earlier differences with Sufis. In 1326 he was again arrested for issuing *fatwas* and held in the Citadel of Damascus until his death three years later. Shortly before his death he was deprived of writing materials, since he had continued to deliver *fatwas* even while in prison. The issue in Damascus, then, was defiance of the sultan's orders, though the *fatwa* of 1326 had been against the visiting of tombs, a practice particularly associated with Sufis.

Although Ibn Taymiya is now remembered as an enemy of Sufism, it was not Sufis but Ibn Taymiya himself who suffered as a result of his views. These views fell into two parts, both deriving from a variety of fundamentalism. As well as denouncing various practices he considered unorthodox, Ibn Taymiya had uncompromising views on the significance of references in the Quran to physical attributes of God: His hands, face, etc. Ibn Taymiya maintained that such references should be taken literally, on the grounds that to seek to interpret the words of the Quran to mean anything other than what the first Muslims had taken them to mean was in effect blasphemous and that the first Muslims had simply listened to what they heard. Although Ibn Taymiya's point was about Quranic exegesis—he did not mean to suggest that God literally had hands in the same way that he himself did—his views were enough to sustain charges of anthropomorphism made against him, and it was for this heresy that he was generally imprisoned.

Ibn Taymiya's views on Quranic exegesis were of little direct relevance to Sufism, but did lead him to disagree emphatically with views that many Sufis held and particularly with those of Ibn al-'Arabi on the Unity of Being. This evidently combined with his attacks on certain Sufi practices to give the appearance of an attack on Sufism as a whole—an appearance against which Ibn Taymiya's persecutors reacted, or perhaps over-reacted. In fact, Ibn Taymiya was not hostile to all and every aspect of Sufism. Although he rejected most of Ibn al-'Arabi he endorsed most of al-Ghazali, for example, and was himself at some point a member of the Qadiriya order. He accepted *wali*s much as everyone else did, opposing only the way they were often treated: some Sufis, he believed, were following shaykhs and *wali*s rather than God. He condemned the visiting of *wali*s' tombs and suggested that dead *wali*s who people thought appeared to them in dreams were normally demons impersonating *wali*s. These denunciations of unorthodox practice seem to have been less important in drawing Sufi fire on Ibn Taymiya than his attacks on Ibn al-'Arabi.

A second important critic of Sufi practices, two and a half centuries later, was the Ottoman Turk, Mehmed Kadizade (1582–1635). Kadizade shared with Ibn Taymiya an early association with Sufism and a legal and scholarly training. Like him, he attacked aspects of Sufism—especially the work of Ibn al-'Arabi—rather than Sufism as such. The main difference between him and Ibn Taymiya was in the conse-

quences of his work. Kadizade was protected rather than persecuted by his sultan (Murad IV), whose presence saved him
from physical assault by enraged Sufis against whom he had
been preaching a high-profile sermon in 1633. This time it
was not the critic of Sufis but ultimately Sufis themselves who
suffered, for almost half a century, along with many other
Ottoman subjects.

Kadizade was more of a puritan than an opponent of
Sufism; not all the practices he objected to were associated with
Sufism. Kadizade condemned Ibn al-'Arabi and the visiting of
tombs of *walis*, as had Ibn Taymiya, and he condemned the use
of music or chanting in *dhikr*, but not the practice of *dhikr* in
itself. Action was taken initially only against members of the
general public. The Ottoman sultan responded to Kadizade's
urgings to act against dubious and unorthodox practices by
closing down coffee houses; those found drinking wine or
smoking tobacco were executed. This was an astonishing act,
since while all Muslims would agree that wine is forbidden,
few would consider execution even a remotely appropriate
penalty for its consumption. Today, smoking and drinking
coffee are regarded in the Islamic world much as they are in
the West; while opinion on tobacco is divided, smoking is
invariably seen as a lesser offense than wine-drinking and is
often considered no offense at all. The view of coffee as forbidden is very much an unusual, minority one.

It was not at first Sufis who suffered from these measures,
but the emphasis of the Kadizadelist movement shifted more
toward anti-Sufism after Kadizade's death and the death of
the sultan who had protected him. During the 1650s,
Kadizade's successor called for the execution of Sufis who
failed to abandon practices such as visiting tombs and the
kinds of *dhikr* Kadizade had condemned and for the destruction of their *zawiyas*. He obtained an order from the Grand

Vizier for the destruction of one Sufi *zawiya*; his followers, many of whom were palace soldiers, attempted to pull down a number of others, but were restrained by order of the senior Ottoman religious dignitary, the Shaykh al-Islam. This kind of public disorder was particularly dangerous while the new sultan was still a child, and so a new Grand Vizier arrested the Kadizadelist leadership in 1656 and banished them to Cyprus. On the death of this Grand Vizier in 1661, however, Kadizadelist influence reasserted itself. The ban on smoking was reintroduced, coffee houses and at least one *wali*'s tomb were demolished, and in 1665 all public performances of Sufi rituals were forbidden. Fortunately for Sufis, the Kadizadelist leader was implicated in the disastrous attack on Vienna in 1683 and as a consequence of this was banished. The following year, Sufis were able to return to their old practices, and subsequent Ottoman sultans were generally patrons rather than opponents of Sufism. Kadizadelist influence continued for some time in remoter areas of the Ottoman empire, however, especially among Turkish soldiers and students.

The third great opponent of Sufi practice was Muhammad ibn 'Abd al-Wahhab (1703–92). Ibn 'Abd al-Wahhab was born on the desolate eastern side of the Arabian peninsula just as the remaining Kadizadelists were causing disorder in cities such as Cairo and Damascus. Like Kadizade, he was more of an extreme puritan than an opponent of Sufism as such. The difference between the two is that while Kadizadelism exercised some influence over the Ottoman state for fifty years, the rise of Wahhabism continues to this day—Wahhabism is the official doctrine of the Kingdom of Saudi Arabia, and Saudi Arabia is a rich country which has spread its own version of Islam across the Islamic world.

Like Ibn Taymiya and Kadizade, Ibn 'Abd al-Wahhab was

a scholar who condemned unorthodox practice. Both his background and his early training were less cosmopolitan, however, and his followers were mostly desert nomads: the tribes which acknowledged the leadership of Muhammad ibn Sa'ud, a local ruler who gave Ibn 'Abd al-Wahhab his protection. His teaching condemned not only visits to tombs, as had Ibn Taymiya and Kadizade, but also their construction, to the extent that when Wahhabi-Saudi forces captured Medina in the early years of the nineteenth century, they demolished part of the Mosque of the Prophet itself. To this day pilgrims who tarry too long by the Prophet's tomb there are moved on by guards with sticks.

Kadizade's anti-Sufism was partial and was part of a larger attack on specific unorthodox practices. Ibn 'Abd al-Wahhab went further in his larger attack, declaring all those who did not actively follow his teachings as unorthodox. In effect, the entire Muslim population of the earth (Sufi or non-Sufi) was classified as unbelievers, with the exception of his own followers. This had the important consequence that, for the Wahhabis, the lives and property of non-Wahhabi Muslims were forfeit. Very considerable bloodshed and plunder accompanied the first Saudi-Wahhabi conquest of the Hijaz, the western side of the Arabian peninsula where Mecca and Medina lie.

The excesses of the Wahhabis in the Hijaz shocked the Muslim world, and an army was despatched from Egypt to repel the invaders. In 1812 this army drove the Saudi-Wahhabi forces back east and defeated them. Before returning across the Red Sea, it deported four hundred leading Saudis and Wahhabis and razed the first Saudi capital (Dir'iya) to the ground. The Hijaz returned to Ottoman control, and Wahhabism lay dormant for almost a century.

At the beginning of the twentieth century, a new Saudi ruler, 'Abd al-'Aziz, established control of the eastern side of the Arabian peninsula. The destruction of the Ottoman empire in the First World War left a vacuum which the Saudi-Wahhabis then filled, conquering Mecca for a second time in 1924 and proclaiming the present Kingdom of Saudi Arabia in 1932. Twentieth-century Wahhabism had mellowed somewhat—abandoning the view of all other Muslims as unbelievers, for example—and, from the beginning of the second conquest of the Hijaz, 'Abd al-'Aziz was careful to avoid any repetition of the excesses which had provoked the reaction which ended the first conquest of that area. Tombs of all sorts were demolished, however, and the teaching of versions of Islam at variance with Wahhabism was banned. Although the Saudi rulers resisted some of the more extreme Wahhabi views, allowing the use of the telegraph and tobacco for example, Mecca was transformed from the great center for the practice and spread of Sufism it had been into a city where Sufi practice can only continue under cover.

Since the changes wrought in Saudi Arabia by the coming of great oil wealth, Wahhabi influence has been spread across the Islamic world by well-funded institutions such as the Saudi-dominated Islamic World League and by subsidized educational programs inside Saudi Arabia, which are attended by many of the future religious leaders of poorer Muslim countries. Not all graduates of such institutions are precisely Wahhabis, but their views are inevitably influenced by Wahhabism, including Wahhabi hostility toward many Sufi practices. Wahhabism, then, was by far the most serious of the three main challenges to Sufis. It still remains a challenge today.

Sufi 'renewers' of Islam

Ibn Taymiya and Kadizade had Sufi backgrounds, and Ibn Taymiya at least may have remained faithful to some variety of Sufism. In a sense, then, Ibn Taymiya may be regarded less as an opponent of Sufism than as someone who wished to reform it. Reform may also be found at the origin of the Kadizadelist movement: Kadizade was inspired by the teachings of Mehmed Birgili (1518–73), an Ottoman who had started as a Sufi but abandoned his shaykh and order for the study of *fiqh* (law) and who thus made the reverse of the journey that al-Ghazali had made. One product of his journey was a book, *Tariqa al-Muhammadiya*. As well as being the inspiration of the Kadizadelists, this text was also probably one of the sources of the Tariqa Muhammadiya movement from which Ahmad ibn Idris's Ahmadiya (discussed above) derived. It has been very widely read, and although it is sometimes taken and used as an anti-Sufi work, it also contains positive recommendations, of which the central one is that the true order (or *tariqa*) is the *umma*, the whole Islamic community. It criticizes certain Sufi practices, but that on its own does not make it anti-Sufi; many Sufis, too, have criticized certain Sufi practices.

Among the Sufis who criticized certain Sufi practices were the founders of the two early orders we considered in Chapter Three. 'Abd al-Qadir al-Jilani's stress on orthodoxy was in part a corrective to the behavior of some Sufis of his time, whose concentration on inner spiritual realities sometimes led them to forget the importance of the external rules of Islam: to forget that balance between the exoteric and the esoteric, which, as we have seen, is central to Sufism. Likewise, al-Shadhili objected to the use of patched cloaks and other external signs of Sufism, and Shadhilis ever since have been publicly more or less anonymous.

Certain Naqshbandi shaykhs have attempted to modify Ibn al-'Arabi's conception of the Unity of Being into a more acceptable Unity of Witnessing. The details of this are com-

97

plicated, but it served to head off some of the attacks on Sufis to which, as we have seen, the complexity of Ibn al-'Arabi's work gave rise. Other shaykhs have observed irregularities which have crept into aspects of Sufism and Islam and attempted to remove them, especially in India, where close contact with non-Muslim Hindus produces a special risk of cross-cultural transmission (or, from an Islamic point of view, infection). Indian Muslims have, for example, at times adopted aspects of the festivals of their Hindu neighbors to a point where their *mawlid*s became more and more like Hindu festivals. Some Indian shaykhs have therefore attempted to return *mawlid*s to what they originally were, often against the opposition of other shaykhs with less purist views.

In other areas, Sufis have criticized more than aspects of Sufi practice. Sufi orders have from time to time arisen which preach the strangest doctrines, in one case going so far as to see their shaykh as an incarnation of God Himself. In these cases, all other Muslims, Sufi or not, have generally joined in shocked condemnation.

Besides being guides on the esoteric path of Sufism, all Sufi shaykhs are to a greater or lesser extent teachers of the exoteric law of Islam. Teaching is never simply a matter of setting forth that which needs to be learned and always involves an element of correcting misconceptions. Misconceptions can arise in a Muslim's understanding of Islam or in a Sufi's understanding of Sufism. In the same way that there have always been disputes among Muslims on a variety of points (usually minor) there have also always been disputes among Sufis on certain matters, the desirability of the use of music in spiritual exercises, for example. Sometimes the same practice may be condemned by a Sufi shaykh and by a critic unconnected to Sufism. It is not in the act of condemnation that opposition to Sufism is to be found, but in the general motivation of the individual in question. Until the modern period, blanket condemnation of all aspects of Sufism has been extremely rare. In the nineteenth and twentieth centuries, however, things have often been different.

The impact of modernity

Different parts of the world of Islam encountered Western modernity at different times and in different ways, and the impact of modernity on Sufism was equally varied. A full survey of these encounters would take many pages; what follows is necessarily much simplified.

Napoleon's landing in Egypt in 1798 is often used as the starting point for a consideration of Islam and modernity, but this date is too late. The Napoleonic expedition may have made a newly scientific and receptive West much more aware of Islam and of Pharaonic Egypt, but Napoleon did not introduce the West to Islam. Christendom and Islam had come into contact with the first Muslim expeditions beyond the Arabian peninsula in the seventh century, and remained in contact ever after. The change that marks the introduction of modernity to Islam is not a change in contact, but a change in attitude.

In the days of Frederick II of Sicily in the early thirteenth century, some Christians—secure in their faith and in the knowledge of their superiority—had recognized that there was much they could learn from the Muslims. Frederick II adorned his splendid court with all the sophistication, both physical and intellectual, that he could import from the Muslim world. As the consequences of the Enlightenment worked their way through Europe, however, the balance between the two civilizations changed. A series of military defeats at the hands of European armies in the sixteenth and seventeenth centuries began to make it clear to the Ottomans that something was wrong, that the West had something important which the Muslims did not have. (It was one of these defeats, incidentally, which had led indirectly to the final suppression of the Kadizadelists in Turkey itself). Many Muslims—secure in their faith and the knowledge of their superiority—now slowly recognized that there was much they had to learn from the Christians. The almost indecent speed with which Napoleon's armies overcame resistance in Egypt served as a graphic illustration of this.

The initial attempt was to learn from the West what was useful—techniques of organization, military tactics—and to protect Islam from what was harmful, from what might weaken Muslims' security in their faith or damage Muslim societies. This objective proved difficult to achieve. Someone who learned French to read an artillery manual could also read Voltaire; someone who visited Paris to pick up ideas for engineering could pick up many other ideas at the same time. Printing was initially allowed by the Ottomans only for technical manuals, but works of history and then books on religion came to be printed, too, and finally so did newspapers, in city after city across the Muslim world. One by one, the ideas and techniques which had slowly introduced modernity in the West reached Islam rather more quickly than they had arrived in the West. In many cases, they were even followed by periods of Western rule.

Salafism and its heirs

One important consequence of the Muslim encounter with modernity was the rise in the late nineteenth century of a variety of movements collectively known (in the West, at least) as 'Salafi.' Varieties of Salafism are to be found almost everywhere, but the central focus of Salafism was a journal published by a Syrian in Cairo. This journal, *al-Manar*, was read by influential 'reformers' as far away as Malaysia, where local Salafis formed a movement known as *Kaum Muda* or

100

'new generation.' These Salafi reformers are in some ways the religious and ideological counterparts of the Young Turks, the modernist activists who seized control of the Ottoman Empire and steered it through defeat in the First World War to its final extinction.

Whether Salafism was primarily a religious or primarily an ideological movement may be disputed. Either way, it was a modernist, 'reformist' movement that expressed itself very much in religious terms. The *Salaf* to whom the Salafis appealed were the '[pious] ancestors,' somewhat hypothetical early Muslims to whose pure practice later Muslims needed to return. The late twentieth-century fundamentalist slogan 'Islam is the solution' (to, by implication, all possible problems) is in origin a Salafi slogan. For Salafis and their fundamentalist heirs, the Islam which is the solution needs to be purified of all impurities and accretions. The Salafis are somewhat reminiscent of the early European Protestants and to some extent arose in response to similar stimuli. In their general orientation toward purification they are also similar to earlier figures such as Ibn Taymiya, but as we will see they are also very different.

Certain characteristics of Salafism are very Protestant. Just as Protestants returned to the Bible to read it for themselves, so Salafis returned to the Quran and likewise ignored centuries of tradition and interpretation in a way which would have appalled Ibn Taymiya. As Protestants railed against the 'superstitious' cult of saints, so did Salafis. The subtleties of Ibn al-'Arabi appealed to the Salafis no more than similar theological niceties had attracted the Protestants. As Protestant European writers ascribed the backwardness of southern Europe to the darkness of Papistry, so Salafis blamed the newly discovered backwardness of the Muslim world on, especially, the Sufis.

101

As Salafism slowly spread through the institutions of Islam from the 1870s to the 1930s, Salafis progressively excluded Sufism and Sufis. The great universities of Islam—the Azhar in Egypt, the Qarawiyin in Morocco—had once been staffed by *ulema* who were often Sufi, and the *ulema* they produced were also often Sufis. While there were still Sufi *ulema* at the Azhar at the end of the twentieth century, they were definitely a minority and they kept tactfully silent about their affiliations. At the start of the nineteenth century, Sufis had been a public majority among the *ulema*. While students at the Azhar today may be Sufis, this is likely to be more despite their attendance at the Azhar than as a result of it.

Just as Sufis were being pushed out of the ranks of the *ulema* by Salafis, the *ulema* themselves were being pushed out of their leading positions in society by the processes of modernization. For centuries, administrators, judges, and sometimes even great merchants had been *ulema*, and the basic meaning of the word lies somewhere between 'educated' and 'scholar.' That the education and scholarship concerned was essentially religious was of much the same significance as the emphasis on classical education in European universities of the eighteenth century. While it had a definite impact on the world-view of the men concerned, it no more made educated Muslims mere 'doctors of the Law' than it made educated Europeans mere classicists. From the mid-nineteenth century, however, administrators, judges, and writers were increasingly trained in new secular institutions. The role of the *ulema* shrank, and their prestige and influence declined as a consequence.

Sufis thus found themselves doubly marginalized. They were losing their position in a group which had once dominated intellectual discourse, and at the same time this group was itself losing its position to elites who favored a different kind of discourse, a more 'modern' discourse. Both the religious discourse (now dominated by Salafis) and the new secular discourse were hostile to Sufism.

The new discourse

The Arabic language itself changed significantly around the end of the nineteenth century. Journalism became increasingly influential, and Arab journalists relied heavily on the European press. Many articles would call for the coining of new words to represent European terms or concepts which until then had no equivalent in Arabic.

One particularly revealing neologism at this time has been spotted by Reinhard Schulze. 'Original' acquired two almost contradictory meanings in Arabic, as it already had in European languages. Is an original idea a new idea, or is it the first idea—that is to say, a very old idea? This linguistic shift marks both a change in attitudes and a complicated and long-drawn-out argument within Islam about the proper place of later interpretations of the 'original' texts. This argument resulted in Salafis putting forth, and many people accepting, a variety of interpretations which were 'original' in the sense of 'novel'—though Salafis, like Protestants before them, claimed that they were also 'original' in the sense of being more correct than the previously accepted interpretations. These 'original' interpretations undermined many of the bases of Sufism.

If 'original' is good, 'traditional'—previously accepted—becomes bad. Authority is questioned, and traditional authorities are rejected. This, too, had serious implications for Sufism and for the traditional authority of the Sufi shaykh. As we have seen, in previous ages individuals and sometimes groups had attacked individual Sufi practices; now, for the first time, the general trend of most Muslim societies was hostile to much that was fundamental to Sufism as a whole. The old objections to Ibn al-'Arabi and the visiting of graves continued, becoming even more serious: in the 1970s, for example, an activist member of the Egyptian parliament succeeded in having the works of Ibn al-'Arabi briefly banned, and an activist village school teacher encouraged his pupils to disrupt the local *mawlid* by stealing candles left at the tomb of a *wali*. More important was a growing view that Sufism was opposed to progress, a cause of backwardness. Modernist intellectuals such as the Pakistani Fazlur Rahman, searching for the causes of the 'decadence' of Islamic civilization, frequently blamed 'un-Islamic' Sufism, "with its auto-hypnotic visions, orgiastic rituals and a motley of superstitious beliefs which further degenerated quite commonly into gross exploitation and charlatanism."

The view of Sufis as backward and primitive has taken different forms in different parts of the Islamic world. In almost all cases, those who hold this view know almost nothing about Sufism. This is easy enough for urban elites who rarely venture out of the modern areas of major cities, since Sufis are nowadays most visible in villages or poor areas of the cities. In many cities, the old centers have become virtual slums. In Cairo, for example, amenities such as running water, electricity, and proper drainage were for many decades available only in the new quarters; the rich abandoned old palaces for villas in these new quarters, and their palaces fell into disrepair and became tenements or ruins. The streets surrounding the great mosques and tombs are now dark and noisy, full of crowds, donkeys, hand carts, and small workshops; the buildings are in a lamentable state of repair, to the extent that architectural gems sometimes simply fall down. The rich and middle classes, who live in modern blocks of flats with satellite television on the other side of town, might very occasionally drive their Japanese cars or their Mercedes down to the old city for a bit of local color, but the rich are more likely to experience 'traditional culture' in the form of sanitized re-creations of a street café in a five-star hotel than by actually venturing into areas which they see as full of disease, crime, and menace.

In Egypt, then, the educated urban elites usually know almost nothing of Sufism, but have a very clear view of what it is: dirty, primitive, irrational, and nothing to do with Islam. In other countries the picture is somewhat different. In contemporary Malaysia, for example, 'Sufism' is commonly taught in schools and universities, but it has been redefined as something which would best be translated into European languages as 'ethics.' Only in a very few countries such as the Sudan does Sufism retain its original prestige.

State intervention

The general hostility of contemporary elites toward Sufism is everywhere a problem for Sufis; the hostility of the state itself has been an even greater problem in some areas. This hostility is not universal—the fundamentalist Sudanese government of Omar al-Bashir and Dr. al-Turabi, for example, sought Sufi support—but the attempt to create modern, powerful states has often had severe consequences for Sufis.

One of the earliest Islamic states to carry through a policy of modernization was Egypt. After Napoleon returned to France having severely disrupted the workings of the Egyptian state, the Ottoman authorities sent an army under a Circassian general, Mehmed Ali, to restore order. Mehmed Ali was so successful in establishing control of Egypt that he saw little need to answer to his erstwhile masters in Istanbul and established a dynasty which ruled Egypt until its last representative, King Farouk, was escorted onto his yacht and into exile in 1952. He and his successors followed a program of centralization of power which echoed the earlier policies of

the Enlightened Despots in Europe. The day-to-day administration of justice, which had previously been largely independent, was brought under government control; the *fiqh* was
ultimately replaced by a version of the Code Napoléon. The
rector of the Azhar university became a state appointee; the
waqf endowments of charitable and educational institutions
were nationalized. Sufis, too, were part of this centralization
program: a state-appointed official was given powers to regu-
late them. This post was transformed by a series of laws into
the presidency of the Supreme Council for Sufi Affairs, which
existed throughout the twentieth century.

In the event, the impact of this official and of the Council
was limited. Many orders and shaykhs simply ignored it;
those which did register (as the law required them to) were
obliged to adopt certain bureaucratic practices, including
membership registers and printed forms of a specified variety
for certain purposes, but were able to continue their religious
activities more or less as they wished. Certain spectacular
public ceremonies which had been exciting the interest of
European visitors were banned, but these affected mostly
only one order, the Rifa'iya. The Supreme Council for Sufi
Affairs intervened periodically in succession disputes,
almost always in favor of the hereditary candidate, which may
have had a slightly deadening effect, but its more grandiose
plans—such as one for harnessing Sufism to the ends of Arab
Socialism, conceived in the early years of the Nasser period—came to nothing.

The Egyptian experience of state intervention reflects the
nature of the Egyptian state: all-powerful in theory, but in
practice often ignored by a population much attached to a
characteristic variety of somewhat anarchic liberty. The
Syrian experience was different. At the beginning of the twentieth century, when Syria was still part of the Ottoman empire,

Sufis benefitted considerably from the Ottoman attempt to reinforce traditional values; subsidies and printing permits were distributed liberally to Sufis. After independence, the tables turned. Sufi orders suffered first expropriation, then persecution, more for political than ideological or religious reasons. Syria is a patchwork of different religious and even ethnic identities, ruled at the end of the twentieth century by an elite drawn from the Alawite minority. The Alawites are fearful and suspicious of the Sunni majority, and any significant Sunni groups are discouraged by the security apparatus. The most ferocious persecution is reserved for fundamentalists—perhaps with some justification, since their aims are avowedly political—but even Sufis are discouraged. Members of even the most apolitical of Sufi orders may be contacted by the security police and 'advised' not to attend *dhikr* any more, advice that some ignore, but which many do not. By the 1990s, one Sufi order reigned supreme over Syria: the Kuftariya, a branch of the Naqshbandiya led by a state official (the Mufti) who received generous state patronage in return for the political and ideological support he gave to the regime.

Perhaps the most dramatic state persecution of Sufis, however, occurred in Turkey. Having saved his nation from the victorious Allies, General Kemal Ataturk turned to its regeneration. This required the obliteration of Ottomanism. The Republic of Turkey was given a new capital and a new language; script and other linguistic reforms mean that, for a Turk of 2000, a book printed in 1910 might as well be written in a foreign language. Ottoman music schools were closed and Ottoman clothing banned by law; the wearing of many kinds of hat could lead to arrest. Islam also was 'reformed,' as Turkey became a 'secular' state in a very special sense: not in the sense of the state's withdrawal from and neutrality in religious matters as is normal in the West, but in the form of an active discouragement of many forms of religious activity, more reminiscent of the official atheism of the Soviet Union. Under certain circumstances prayer became a criminal offense; for a brief period it was even forbidden to give the call to prayer in Arabic. This was the equivalent of forbidding the use of Latin in the mass in the days before the Second Vatican Council. Unsurprisingly in these circumstances, Sufism was 'abolished.'

The Turkish abolition of Sufism could not, of course, extirpate it entirely, and by the end of the twentieth century a compromise of sorts had been reached. Jalal al-Din Rumi, the shaykh who founded the Mevleviya order, for example, is officially described as a 'philosopher,' and his tomb in Konya is now a state-run 'museum.' It is possible to visit his tomb after buying a ticket, though a kind official will sometimes exempt a pilgrim from this formal requirement. There are few other museums in the world which people commonly enter in order to pray, in a room containing glass cases and even a few genuine tourists, but the appearance of secularism is maintained. *Zawiya*s continue to function on new premises, and rumors circulate of the Naqshbandiya order's secret power. Modern Turkey's intellectual and other elites may regard Sufism with something that at times approaches fascinated horror, but Sufism survives.

Sufism in partial eclipse

Sufism, then, began as a practice without a name, as the battle of individuals against their *nafs* in the greater *jihad*. It developed theorists and orders; orders rose, spread, declined, and were replaced; and the list of great shaykhs and *walis* grew longer and longer. Sufis became involved in trade and politics and warfare, and in the administration of Islam as scholars, lawyers, and preachers. Then, after more than a millennium, the mainstream that Sufis had inhabited turned; political, social, and economic changes forced Sufism out, making it in some instances almost a sect within Islam, sometimes even a persecuted one.

At the end of the twentieth century, Sufism was in partial eclipse in the Islamic world—ironically, just as it was beginning to spread in the West, in the civilization whose earlier expansion was instrumental in the turn in the mainstream which marginalized Sufism in the Islamic world. Sufis are now more likely to be found in villages than in universities, on public buses or on foot than in airplanes. The tombs of great *wali*s are falling into disrepair, and the future of the Islamic world is debated between fundamentalism and materialism. What future does Sufism have?

Most Sufis would reply to such a question by asking what future the world has. For Sufis, the eclipse of Sufism is synonymous with the eclipse of true religion, and once true religion has almost vanished from the world, the Final Day will come, as countless *hadith* predict and explain. Millenarian expectations have always been popular among Muslims, but are particularly widespread today among Sufis, many of whom would be not at all surprised to see the Day of Judgment in their own lifetimes.

Some Sufis, however, have attempted to adjust to contemporary conditions. In some cases this may mean little more than giving an acceptable public face to their orders—renaming them 'associations,' for example, or stressing much the same activities that other Islamic organizations stress: education, the provision of medical services to the poor, Islamic unity. Often a Sufi order on more or less the normal pattern is to be found behind such a facade. Sometimes, however, a Sufi order has actually changed its inner identity in response to circumstances. One section of the Ahmadiya, the origins of which were

109

discussed in Chapter Three, has, for example, attempted to map out a 'third way' between Sufism and Salafism, transforming itself from a Sufi order into a 'Family.' Many of the trappings of Sufism have been removed—the title 'shaykh' forbidden, the emphasis on *dhikr* reduced, anything resembling *majdhub* abhorred. Ethical values from mutual cooperation to cleanliness are instead emphasized, as is education.

This 'third way' has had some success in attracting people who would otherwise have had little interest in anything connected to Sufism and might rather have become Salafis, if not fundamentalists. Many of its followers, however, stick obstinately to their original conception of Sufism, finding various ways to ignore the changes which have taken place in their order. For these people, those aspects of Sufism which depend little upon the shaykh continue much as normal. For others, the 'Family' is significant in their spiritual lives, but has a significance different from the Sufism which this book has presented. This 'third way,' then, and some others as well, could be seen to adapt Sufism to the modern world at the expense of what is essentially Sufi, and so as showing that Sufism and the modern world are not really compatible.

Sufism, however, remains, as do shaykhs and *wali*s. For those who wish to follow it, the esoteric path which Sufis trace back to the Prophet is still there, even if it has to be looked for more carefully than in past centuries. Sufism survives its partial eclipse, numerically diminished perhaps, but offering the individual seeker the same possibilities that it always has.

Some of the *Hikam* of Ibn 'Ata Allah

What follows is an inevitably personal selection of some of the 262 *hikam* or sayings of Ibn 'Ata Allah al-Sakandari (for whom and for the origin of whose work, see Chapter Three). On the whole, I have avoided *hikam* which are lengthy or which refer to complex concepts not covered in this short book; I have chosen particularly those which appealed to me personally or which illuminated themes developed above.

Although arranged as a book, the *hikam* can hardly be read as a book—that would be an excessively rich diet. Even a small selection such as that which follows may best be read at several sittings.

The translations are based on those by Victor Danner (see bibliography in Appendix Three).

And he said (may God be pleased with him!):

- Bury your existence in the earth of obscurity, for whatever sprouts forth without having first been buried, flowers imperfectly.
- The cosmos is all darkness and is illuminated only by the manifestation of God in it. Whoever sees the cosmos and does not contemplate Him in it or by it or before it or after it is in need of light, and is veiled from the sun of *'irfan* [gnosis] by the clouds of created things.

He who wishes that at a given moment there appear other than what God has manifested in it, has not left ignorance behind at all.

- Your postponement of deeds until the time when you are free is one of the frivolities of the *nafs*.

- Not a breath [*nafs*] do you expire but a decree of destiny has made it go forth.

- So long as you are in this world, do not be surprised at the existence of sorrows, for truly it manifests nothing but what is in keeping with its character and inevitable nature.

- Among the signs of success at the end is turning to God at the beginning.

- The source of every disobedience, indifference, and passion is self-satisfaction. The source of every obedience, vigilance, and virtue is dissatisfaction with one's self. It is better for you to keep company with an ignorant man dissatisfied with himself than to keep company with a learned man satisfied with himself. For what knowledge is there in a self-satisfied scholar? And what ignorance is there in an unlearned man dissatisfied with himself?

- Do not keep company with anyone whose state does not inspire you and whose speech does not lead you to God.

- Let no sin reach such proportions in your eyes that it cuts you off from having a good opinion of God, for whoever knows his Lord considers his sin as paltry next to His generosity.

- In your despairing you are a free man, but in your coveting you are a slave.

- Infer the existence of ignorance in anyone whom you see answering all that he is asked or giving expression to all that he witnesses or mentioning all that he knows.

- Sometimes He gives while depriving you, and sometimes He deprives you in giving.

- If you want a glory that does not vanish, then do not glory in a glory that vanishes.

- Suffice it as a recompense to you for your obedience that He has judged you worthy of obedience.
- A disobedience that bequeaths humiliation and extreme need is better than an obedience that bequeaths self-infatuation and pride.
- When He alienates you from His creatures, then know that He wants to open for you the door of intimacy with Him.
- When the forgetful man gets up in the morning, he thinks about what he is going to do; the intelligent man sees what God is doing with him.
- Were the light of certitude to shine, you would see the hereafter so near that you could not move toward it, and you would see that the eclipse of extinction had come over the beauties of the world.
- People praise you for what they suppose is in you, but you must blame your soul for what you know is in it.
- Sometimes you will find more benefit in states of need than you find in fasting or in ritual prayer.
- Every utterance that comes forth does so with the vestments of the heart from which it issued.
- When two matters seem confusing to you, see which is heavier on the *nafs* and follow it through—for nothing weighs on the *nafs* but what is true.
- He made service of Him obligatory for you, which is to say that He made entrance into His paradise obligatory for you.
- Incurable sickness results when the sweetness of passion takes possession of the heart.
- So that your sadness over something be little, let your joy in it be little.
- He knew you would not accept mere counsel, so He made you sample the world's taste to a degree that separation from it would be easy for you.

- If fear is united with knowledge, then it is for you; if not, then it is against you.
- He only made affliction come at the hands of people so that you repose not in them. He wanted to drive you out of everything so that nothing would divert you from Him.
- So long as you have not contemplated the Creator, you belong to created beings; but when you have contemplated Him, created beings belong to you.

Glossary

Azhari A scholar / member of the *ulema* educated at the ancient and prestigious Azhar university-mosque in Cairo.

Baraka Blessings, divinely-derived spiritual power, or divine grace. See Chapter Two.

Bedouin Nomads; dwellers in the desert.

Dars A lesson, especially one given on a formal occasion by a shaykh to a group of Sufis who have gathered to hear it. May be extempore or formal, based on a text.

Dervish In European languages, a Sufi. Actually the Europeanized form of *darwish*, a poor man; equivalent to the Arabic *faqir*. Hence a Sufi belonging to an order (qv) which emphasizes voluntary poverty.

Dhikr Repetitive prayer with the objective of 'remembering' (being always mindful of) God. When performed in a group, a distinctively Sufi ceremony. See Chapter Two.

Esoteric Relating to the internal realities of religion, man's personal experience of the divine, etc.

Exoteric Relating to the external practices of religion, such as worship or ethics.

Fatwa The expression of the considered opinion of an expert on a question of law or religious practice. This opinion is expected to be persuasive, but is not legally binding or enforceable.

Fiqh Law; the codified parts of the *Shari'a* (qv).

Give To 'give' an order (qv) is to admit into the order the person who 'takes' it (qv).

Hadith Reports of the words or actions of the Prophet or, sometimes, of his companions. *Hadith* are one of the two main sources from which the *Shari'a* of Islam is derived, the other being the Quran (qv).

Hijra A migration, especially the migration of the Prophet and his companions from Mecca to Medina in year one of the Islamic calendar (A.D. 622).

'Irfan Knowledge, especially direct knowledge of God; illumination; one description of the end of the Sufi path.

Islam The religion taught by the Prophet Muhammad and contained in the Quran (qv) as a result of what Muslims believe to be the last in a series of divine revelations. Islam perfects and replaces the two preceding divine revelations, of Christianity through Jesus and of Judaism through Moses. Hence Islamic: of or relating to the religion of Islam.

Jihad Struggle, war, especially the 'greater' *jihad* against one's *nafs* (qv) or the 'lesser' *jihad* against the enemies of the Muslims, in which case *jihad* in practice often means 'military service.' *Jihad*, however, differs from conscription in that it involves an element of voluntary sacrifice.

Khalifa Heir, successor. The leaders of the Muslims after the death of the Prophet were the Prophet's *khalifa*s; hence, 'Caliph,' one of the titles of later rulers such as the Ottoman sultan. In Sufism, the successor or, more usually, the authorized representative of a shaykh (qv).

Khalwa Retreat (see Chapter Two). In Sudanese usage, a Sufi settlement including a school.

Mawlid The anniversary of a *wali* (qv) and thus the celebration of that anniversary, usually at the tomb of the *wali* in question.

Muslim One who has accepted (literally, 'submitted to') Islam. As an ad-jective, properly applied only to persons. Being Muslim is one stage below being *mu'min*, a believer, i.e. refers more to civil status than to spiritual state.

Nafs The lower self (literally, 'breath'). Not the soul. See Chapter One.

Order A group of Sufis sharing some allegiance, however connected otherwise; an imprecise term used to translate the Arabic *tariqa*. The word is applied both to the immediate followers of a particular shaykh (qv), who may be as few as a dozen, or to all the followers of all the shaykhs who 'take' from (qv) an earlier shaykh, for example, al-Shadhili (for whom see Chapter Three). In the latter case, the members of the order will often be in the millions, with no significant organizational links between them.

Prophet The Prophet Muhammad, through whom Muslims believe God revealed the Quran (qv) and established Islam.

117

Although entirely human, the Prophet is considered to be the most perfect of all God's created be-ings, and for many Sufis has a special cosmological significance. The normal Arabic term, *rasul*, is closer in meaning to 'emissary' or 'messenger.'

Quran The collection of all God's revelations to the Prophet (qv). Muslims believe that the words of the Quran are entirely of divine origin, the only human agency involved being the first speaking of them by the Prophet and then the first recording of them by various companions of the Prophet. The Quran was revealed over a period of years, taking its final organizational form only after the death of the Prophet. Given its origin outside time and creation, Muslims regard the Quran as being entirely different from anything else on earth.

Salafism A nineteenth-century Islamic reform movement akin to Protestantism in Christianity. See Chapter Five.

Shari'a The detail of the religion of Islam (qv); how a Muslim (qv) should live, in the widest sense. It includes the *fiqh* (qv), but also rules and principles (often the *sunna* [qv]) which cannot properly be called law. Often misused to mean only the *fiqh*.

Shaykh An old or respected man, especially a learned one; a scholar or ruler. In Sufism, a master; the one whom a number of Sufis follow.

Silsila The chain of succession linking a shaykh (qv) to the Prophet (qv). See Chapter Two.

Sufi A Muslim (qv) who follows the esoteric (qv) path within Islam (qv), usually by following a Sufi shaykh (qv).

Sunna Tradition, particularly certain traditions established by the words and actions of the Prophet (qv). Hence, Sunni (qv). Something which is *sunna* is not required by the *fiqh* (qv), but although not incumbent on a Muslim (qv) is recommended. For example, it is *sunna* to put the right foot forward when entering a mosque.

Sunni Following the *sunna*; used to distinguish the majority of Muslims from the Shia, a distinct and in some ways distinctive group now forming the majority in Iran and sizeable minorities in many other countries from Iraq to Syria.

Take To 'take' an order (qv) is to join oneself to the *silsila* (qv) of a shaykh (qv); alternatively, a Sufi becomes a Sufi by 'taking from' a shaykh. The concept is often denoted in European languages by 'initiation,' but this word has a variety of connotations not present in Sufism, even though it often marks the beginning of a Sufi's ascent of the spiritual path.

Tekke A *zawiya* (qv), Turkish.

Traditionalism An early twentieth-century religious and philosophical movement originating in France. See Chapter Three.

Ulema Scholars, especially scholars learned in Islam (qv), especially in the *fiqh* (qv) and the exoteric (qv) aspects of the *Shari'a* (qv). Thus, the general class of exoteric religious scholars.

Umma The total community of all the Muslims (qv).

119

Unity of Being A conception given its classic expression by Ibn al-'Arabi (and subscribed to by many Sufis) which describes the relationship between the Creator and His creation. See Chapter Three.

Wahhabi An eighteenth-century Islamic reform movement akin to extreme Puritanism in Christianity. See Chapter Five.

Wali One whom God favors, one who is close to God; akin in some ways to a saint in Christianity. See Chapter Two.

Wird The extra practices, particularly prayers and individual *dhikr* (qv). which a Sufi is instructed to perform (usually daily) by his shaykh (qv).

Zawiya A small building or even room set aside for prayer; hence, in Sufism, the premises used or occupied by an order (qv). The word may also indicate the Sufis using a particular *zawiya*, rather as the term 'lodge' indicates a group of freemasons.

Bibliography

Works by Sufis

Classic works

The works of al-Ghazali and Ibn al-'Arabi are immense, and only a fraction of them has been translated into any European language. These and most other works given here are theological in nature, whether in prose or in verse.

There are more than fifty different compilations of Rumi's poetry currently in print in English. Those suggested below are older and more scholarly translations; many more literary translations will be found with ease in most bookstores.

Attar, Farid-Ud-Din. *The Conference of the Birds*. Penguin, 1984.

Chittick, William C., ed. *Faith and Practice of Islam: Three Thirteenth Century Sufi Texts*. State University of New York Press, 1992.

Ad-Darqawi, Al-Arabi. *Letters of a Sufi Master: The Shaykh ad-Darqawi*. Trans. Titus Burckhardt. Fons Vitae, 1998.

Al-Ghazali, Abu Hamid. *Deliverance from Error and Mystical Union with the Almighty: Al-Munqidh min al-dalal*. Trans. George F. McLean. Council for Research in Values and Philosophy, 2000.

———. *The Remembrance of Death and the Afterlife: Kitab dhikr al-mawt wa ma badahu* [Book XL of the *Revival of the Religious Sciences, Ihya 'ulum al-din*]. Trans. T. J. Winter. Islamic Texts Society, 1989.

Al-Haddad, Abdallah ibn Alawi. *The Book of Assistance*. Trans. Mostafa al-Badawi. The Quilliam Press, 1989.

Al-Jilani, 'Abd al-Qadir. *Utterances of Shaikh 'Abd al-Qadir al-Jilani [Malfuzat].* Trans. Muhtar Holland. Al-Baz Publishing, 1992.

———. *The Removal of Cares [Jala' al-khawatir].* Al-Baz Publishing, 1997.

———. *Necklaces of Gems [Qala'id al-jawahir].* Ed. Muhammad ibn Yahya at-Tadifi. Trans. Muhtar Holland. Al-Baz Publishing, 1998

Ibn al-Arabi, Muhyi al-Din. *Journey to the Lord of Power: A Sufi Manual on Retreat.* Inner Traditions International, 1989.

———. *Divine Governance of the Human Kingdom, Including What the Seeker Needs and The One Alone.* Mass Market Paperbacks, 1997.

———. *Islamic Sainthood in the Fullness of Time: Ibn Al-Arabi's Book of the Fabulous Gryphon.* Ed. Gerald T. Elmore. Brill, 1999.

———. *Mysteries of Purity: Ibn Al-Arabi's Asrar al-taharah.* Trans. Eric Winkel. Crossroads, 1996.

Ibn 'Ata' Allah. *The Book of Wisdom.* Trans. Victor Danner. Published in one volume with Abdullah Ansari, *Intimate Conversations.* Paulist Press, 1988.

Rumi, Djalal al-Din. *Tales of Mystic Meaning: Selections from the Mathnawi of Jalal-Ud-Din Rumi.* Trans. R. A. Nicholson. Oneworld Publications, 1995.

———. *Rumi's Divan of Shems of Tabriz: Selected Odes.* Trans. James Cowan and R. A. Nicholson. Element, 1997.

———. *The Sufi Path of Love: The Spiritual Teachings of Rumi.* Trans. William C. Chittick. State University of New York Press, 1983.

Sells, Michael A., ed. *Early Islamic Mysticism: Sufi, Quran, Miraj, Poetic and Theological Writings.* Paulist Press, 1996.

Modern Works

The following works are a small selection of what is available and derive mostly from Sufi orders established in the U.S. Two authors (Javad Nurbaksh and Maghsoud Angha) are especially interesting because they represent Shi'i orders (the Nimutallahi and the Oveyssi).

Many Sufi orders in the U.S. have extensive websites, some of which allow on-line book purchase. Most of these websites are linked and classified on the Sufism Page maintained by Alan Godlas of the University of Georgia: http://www.arches.uga.edu/~godlas/Sufism.html.

Al-Jerrahi, Muzaffer Ozak. *Love is the Wine*. Philosophical Research Society, 1999.
————. *Irshad: Wisdom of a Sufi Master*. Pir Publications, 1992.
Angha, Maghsoud Sadegh-Ibn Mohammad. *Al-Salat: The Reality of Prayer in Islam*. MTO Shahmaghsoudi, 1998.
————. *The Fragrance of Sufism*. MTO Shahmaghsoudi, 1997.
Chishti, Hakim Moinuddin. *The Book of Sufi Healing*. Inner Traditions International, 1991.
Kabbani, Muhammad Hisham. *The Naqshbandi Sufi Way: History and Guidebook of the Saints of the Golden Chain*. Kazi, 1995.
————. *Angels Unveiled: A Sufi Perspective*. Kazi, 1996.
Nurbaksh, Javad. *Discourses on the Sufi Path*. Khaniqahi Nimutallahi Publications, 1996.
Wilcox, Lynn. *Women and the Holy Quran: A Sufi Perspective*. MTO Shahmaghsoudi, 1998.

Works by Traditionalists

Some of the Traditionalist works given below are overtly Sufi, some on Islam and some on other religions. Traditionalist books on Islam take such a Sufi approach that they might fairly be described as Sufi books. All these books are to a greater or lesser extent informed by Traditionalist views, but they are also Sufi works, especially the two books of Martin Lings (Sidi Abu Bakr).

Burckhardt, Titus. *An Introduction to Sufi Doctrine*. Kazi, 1976.

Guénon, René. *The Crisis of the Modern World* (1927). Kazi, 1996.

———. *The Reign of Quantity & the Signs of the Times* (1945). Perennial Books, 1995.

———. *East and West* (1924). Perennial books, 1995.

———. *Introduction to the Study of the Hindu Doctrines* (1921). South Asia Books, 1993.

Lings, Martin. *A Sufi Saint of the Twentieth Century: Shaikh Ahmad Al-Alawi: His Spiritual Heritage and Legacy* (1961). Islamic Texts Society, 1993.

———. *What Is Sufism?* Islamic Texts Society, 1999.

Nasr, Seyyed Hossein. *Man and Nature: The Spiritual Crisis in Modern Man*. Kazi, 1997.

———. *Traditional Islam in the Modern World*. Kegan Paul International, 1995

Schuon, Frithjof. *Understanding Islam*. World Wisdom Books, 1998.

———. *Transcendent Unity of Religions*. Quest Books, 1984.

Neo-Sufism

Dervish, H.B.M. *Journeys With a Sufi Master* [Idries Shah]. ISHK Book Service, 1987.

Khan, Inayat. *Awakening: A Sufi Experience*. J.P. Tarcher, 1999.

———. *Sufi Teachings*. Omega, 1991.

Lewis , Samuel L. *Sufi Vision and Initiation: Meetings with Remarkable Beings*. Sirs Caravan Publishers, 1986.

Shah, Idries. *The Way of the Sufi*. Arkana, 1991.

———. *Learning How to Learn: Psychology and Spirituality in the Sufi Way*. Penguin, 1996.

———. *Knowing How to Know: A Practical Philosophy in the Sufi Tradition*. Octagon, 1998.

Works by scholars

General works

Nicholson's introduction to Sufism and Spencer Trimingham's survey are classic works which are now inevitably somewhat dated.

Baker, Rob and Gray Henry. *Sufi Orders, Lineages, and Saints: A Comprehensive Guide*. Fons Vitae, 2000.

Nicholson, Reynold Alleyne. *Studies in Islamic Mysticism*. Curzon Press, 1994.

Schimmel, Annemarie. *Mystical Dimensions of Islam*. University of North Carolina Press, 1985.

Spencer Trimingham, J. *The Sufi Orders in Islam*. Oxford University Press, 1998.

Works on specific orders or figures

Several scholars have written on early great Sufis—Ibn al-'Arabi, Hallaj, and Rumi—and a selection of the best of these are given below. Other figures and orders are somewhat randomly covered by books currently available. Those given below, which deal with Sufism in Africa and India, and the Sanusiya and the Mevleviya, serve however to give some varied flavors to the interested reader.

Addas, Claude. *Quest for the Red Sulphur: The Life of Ibn Arabi*. Islamic Texts Society, 1996.

Arberry, A. J. *The Life and Work of Jalal-Ud-Din Rumi.* Oxford University Press, 1999.

Brenner, Louis. *West African Sufi: The Religious Heritage and Spiritual Quest of Cerno Bokar Saalif Taal.* University of California Press, 1984.

Buehler, Arthur F. *Sufi Heirs of the Prophet: The Indian Naqshbandiyya and the Rise of the Mediating Sufi Shaykh.* University of South Carolina Press, 1998.

Chodkiewicz, Michel. *An Ocean Without Shore: Ibn Arabi, the Book, and the Law.* State University of New York Press, 1993.

Ernst, Carl W. *The Eternal Garden: Mysticism, History, and Politics at a South Asian Sufi Center.* State University of New York Press, 1992.

Friedlander, Shems. Rumi and *the Whirling Dervishes: Being an Account of the Sufi Order Known as the Mevlevis and its Founder the Poet and Mystic Mevlana Jalalu'ddin Rumi.* Parabola Books, 2003.

Knysh, Alexander D. *Ibn 'Arabi in the Later Islamic Tradition: The Making of a Polemical Image in Medieval Islam.* State University of New York Press, 1998.

Lewisohn, Leonard, ed. *The Heritage of Sufism.* Volume one: *Classical Persian Sufism from Its Origins to Rumi (700–1300).* Volume two: *The Legacy of Medieval Persian Sufism (1150–1500).* Element, 1999.

Massignon, Louis. *The Passion of Al-Hallaj; Mystic and Martyr of Islam.* Princeton University Press, 1994.

Schimmel, Annemarie. *The Triumphal Sun: A Study of the Works of Jalaloddinn Rumi.* State University of New York Press, 1993.

Vikør, Knut S. *Sufi and Scholar on the Desert Edge: Muhammad B. Ali Al-Sanusi and His Brotherhood.* Northwestern University Press, 1995.

126